Alchemy Arts
recycling is chic

Published in 2010 in Great Britain and the United States by

MARION BOYARS PUBLISHERS LTD

24 Lacy Road, London SW15 1NL

www.marionboyars.co.uk

Distributed in Australia and New Zealand by Scribo Ltd

18 Rodborough Road, Frenchs Forest, NSW 2086 Australia

Printed in 2009

10 9 8 7 6 5 4 3 2 1

A CIP catalogue record for this book is available from the British Library.
A CIP catalog record for this book is available from the Library of Congress.

ISBN 978-0-7145-3200-4

Set in Linotype Univers 45 Light; size 9.25pt.

Printed by Toppan Leefung, China

Cover and book design by Anna Chapman at www.fogbank.co.uk

Photography by D.N. Anderson at www.dnanderson.co.uk and Fraser Morgan

Hair and make-up by Sarah Spears at www.sarahspears.co.uk

Alchemy Arts
recycling is chic

Kate MacKay and Di Jennings

MARION BOYARS PUBLISHERS
London · New York

'To all the strong women who have taught and
inspired me, from Dolly to little Daisy.'
Kate MacKay

'To my Beloved Guru and World Friend,
Avatar Adi Da Samraj, my Compass and Resort.'
Di Jennings

Contents

Alchemy Arts

A CHANCE MEETING in a café between two women who share a love of art, community, red wine and 1920s ballet costumes has led us on an incredible and inspiring creative journey. We quickly became firm friends and co-conspirators in developing projects that involve the transformation of rubbish into beautiful objects and costumes.

We felt called to inspire others to see the potential carnival in their rubbish bin and so the seed for *Alchemy Arts: Recycling is Chic* was planted. We were inspired and transformed ourselves into working bees to develop our ideas. A flurry of creativity ensued: cutting, stitching and gluing, begging, borrowing and stealing spiralled into parading, performing and posing! The artists, dancers and models within us soon emerged. It was contagious… We were embarking on a celebration of the enjoyment of the abundance that is all around us; having fun finding the inner glamour puss and creating 'a silk purse from a sow's ear'.

In this way the book has developed organically. It has been a coming-together of friends and artists, creative and inspirational people who support and encourage each other to create beauty anywhere from anything. Since we began putting the book together I have heard so much about people being resourceful and creative with all that makes up their lives and environment. The project has turned into a cross-continental collaboration, with many connections made through stories shared. It's amazing how much we find we have in common with other artists across different generations and cultures. Much excited correspondence has bounced across the globe about favourite artists, songs we love and places we remember. Once you start exploring the creative network the world seems to become smaller and more infinite all at once!

We truly feel that creativity can profoundly enhance the way we view ourselves and the world around us. It is empowering to sense that everything is in a cycle of flux; that through the transformation of perceptions and materials, we have the potential to redefine our sense of self, of others and our environment.

And this is just the beginning. We have included the contact details for all the artists in their profiles at the end of the book, so get in touch, join in, show us what you have made, tell us what you think and be part of a new creative adventure – we'd love to hear from you!

Kate MacKay and Di Jennings
www.alchemyarts.org

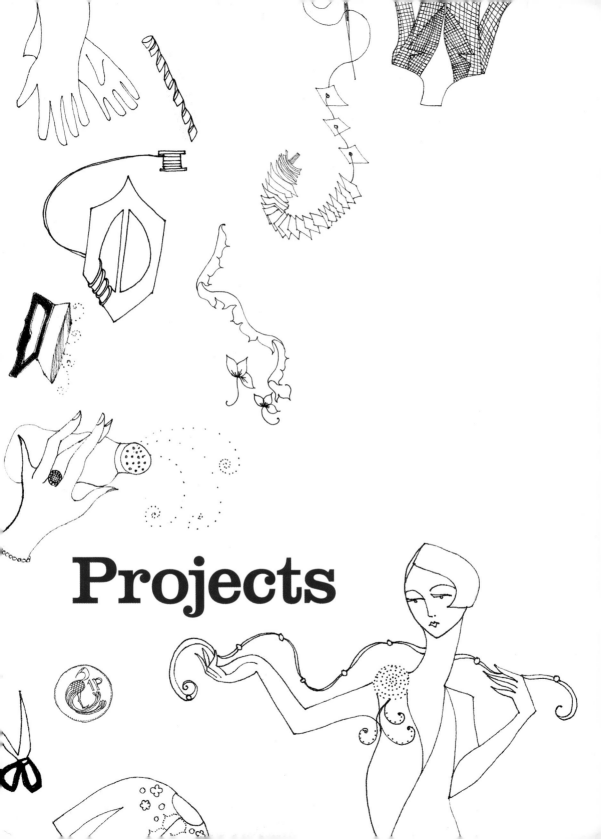

Projects

Chapter 1:

Corsets and Petticoats

'I collected old ties from charity shops, placing geometrics, florals and colourways together'

All Tied Up

DWINDLING CUSTOM caused by increased sobriety in gentlemen's clubs during prohibition gave rise to a new inventiveness when facilitating conversation. Many social zimmers that thrive today were conceived in this setting; games such as the ever-popular charades and 'I spy…' would not have come into being were it not for the lack of brandy. A once popular past-time that did not make the transition was the little known 'cravat roulette'; in fact its existence was rare and fleeting, clashing as it did with the puritanical politics of the era.

The game consisted of a burlesque dancer, saloon girl or local wench dressed entirely in gentlemen's cravats. One-by-one the club members would be called forth to select a cravat from the mademoiselle's garb, which he would tie around his neck in a manner different to his predecessor. The rule was that never should the same knot be tied twice or the game was over, the gentleman shamed and the petticoat left unrevealed. A referee was in place to ensure that all knots were genuine but many expert bluffers actually saw their faux tie knots pass into men's fashion for real. These were known as 'cravat red herrings' later to be abbreviated to 'kippers', one of the few existing references to cravat roulette still used in modern parlance.

The introduction of the longer slimmer tie that is favoured these days directly correlates with the decline of cravat roulette. The game became dull as on a piece-by-piece basis, these modern ties revealed too little of the undergarment at a time, so the game was over too quickly as there are only really one or two ways of knotting them. These slim ties are still known as the 'four in hand' because frustrated gents would often try to tear off several at once in a bid to spice things up a bit.

Our design is a modern take on this little piece of history; we have used the modern 'four in hand' tie, a descendent of the cravat and, of course, ours are firmly stitched in place.

Kate MacKay

Design

I have always loved men's ties, and have used them in many different ways over the years. I made my first skirt from ties around thirty years ago and it was such a favourite that I wore it until it was threadbare. The memories of how fabulous I used to feel in that old tie skirt when I was a single gal got me started on this creation. I collected patterned ties in shades of blue and yellow and started to play with them. I wanted to make something that was both wearable and fun. The ties are attached to an old petticoat that provides the base. I have always been a fan of empire line dresses. They are so elegant and easy to wear – even after dinner!

Di Jennings

Materials: frock

Second-hand stores, jumble sales and hand-me-downs

15 ties
Full length petticoat

Craft supplies

Needle and thread

Materials: headdress

Second-hand stores, jumble sales and hand-me-downs

1 bright patterned tie

Craft supplies

Needle and thread

TIP:
How to make a petticoat-based frock

I collected old ties that I liked from charity shops and jumble sales. Then I grouped them in various formations placing geometrics, florals and colourways together. This dress used about fifteen ties in shades of yellow and blue. For the base, I used an old petticoat.

To make the skirt, I unpicked thirteen of the ties, removed the inside stiffening and then ironed them flat. Then I sewed them together so that the wider V-shape at the end of the ties created the hem at the bottom of the skirt. I turned the petticoat inside out so that the wrong side was facing me and attached the skirt to the petticoat just below the bust. To finish the hem, I trimmed the bottom of the petticoat and hand stitched a small hem so that it could not be seen below the ties.

I used the remnants of the ties to create the bodice (waste not, want not!). This was the tricky bit as I was covering a rounded shape. I find that it is much easier working on a dressmaker's dummy, but did not have one at this time so there was a lot of fiddling around in front of the mirror. I suggest that you ask a good friend to be your model…but insist that she wears a bra to avoid getting stabbed in the bosom! Carefully pin and then hand stitch the bodice pieces together, attaching them to the petticoat as you work. Use another tie to make the two straps and a final tie to cover all the raggedy joins under the bust. Hand stitch the final tie in place over all the ragged edges and it will cover a multitude of sins!

TIP:
How to make
the tie headdress

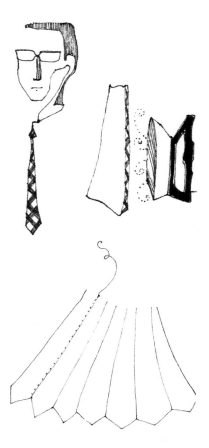

The intention was to make a simple headpiece that had a 1920s feel. The tie headdress is made of three components: a headband, a bow and a hanging 'ribbon'. I could have tied the bow and hanging piece from one length of a tie in a conventional bow, but it would have been bulky, so I decided to proceed as follows…

1   To make the headband, I measured the circumference of my head and cut a length of tie (at the narrower end) to this measurement plus a seam allowance. I overlapped the ends and hand stitched them in place. The stitching is hidden in the final headdress as it is covered with the bow.

2   To make the bow, I cut the tie twice the length of the bow (about 4 inches or 10cm) plus an overlap for the seam allowance. I overlapped the ends and stitched them in place to form a small circle. To make the middle of the bow, I wrapped a small piece of tie fabric (about ½ inch or 1½cm wide) around the centre of the bow and hand stitched this in place at the back.

3   For the hanging 'ribbon', I cut the desired length, using the existing V-shaped end at one end and creating a similar V-shape at the other end by cutting and hand stitching. To finish the headpiece, I folded the 'ribbon' over the headband to cover the hand stitching with one end hanging a little longer than the other. Then I hand stitched the bow in place, I like the bow worn at the side of the head, but it could be worn at the back.

Di Jennings

Roses and Ruffles

> Add a little Parisian romance to your world, with a dress made from a 1930s vintage corset

Roses and Ruffles

1900s PARIS: A SEA OF SILK, LACE AND FRILLS, feathered heads and stockinged legs is centre stage at the Moulin Rouge. Eyes heavy with absinthe perceive the mass as a whirling windmill of roses and carnations poised on poisonous black stalks, heels kicking like thorns. Gone are the solo artistes of yesterday, famed for their suggestive stage names and specialised skills; the athletic Ninni Pettes-en-l'Air with her spinning wheels of steel and the beguiling Mme Forage with her bovine baby bell cheeks, not to mention the enthralling scissor strikes of La Goalie and the elephantine strength and fey flirtation of the riveting Grille d'Evout. All are now lost, amalgamated into the throng of thunderous thighs and provocative petticoats.

The new industrial era favours multitude over singularity and the dancers whirr with precision like cogs and wheels in a factory of fantasy. An ever-expanding workforce marches in, kicking and tapping in synchronised lines. Before long, the brightly lit stage is far more populated than the shadowy floor, men sallow with addiction and propped up by bottles are hallowed by this altar of angels moving en masse, a thousand petticoats are no match for the dizzying height of these kicks. The dandies about to be deceived are no match for these dancers either, though they may be affronted by the syphilis-defying scented silks.

Crowned with perfumed plumes from new exotic climes, it seems that the ostrich, peacock and paradise birds have infiltrated the usual habitat of Parisian sparrows, pigeons and the lark. Slit-knickers hang on harnesses from their girdles; this optimal if vulgar solution to increased production of provocation attracts a less–discerning monocled eye. Multiplicity masks a multitude of sins and the can-can girls are a flawless array of the feminine form. Azure eyes and ruby lips are the war paint of this terrifying and hypnotic army spinning in sinful motion like the hands of a clock. The voyeur's cravat-wrapped neck stoops under the weight of his bowler hat and in that smoky moment, his mortality and transience is emphasised by the bitter absinthe.

Kate MacKay

Design

'Every act of creation is first of all an act of destruction,'
Pablo Picasso

Although I hadn't really thought about it before reading this quote, I realised the truth of the above statement when I related it to my work. There are definite stages of kindness, destruction and creation associated with what I do.

I love working with pretty vintage clothes… pieces that have had a full life and brought joy to the wearer. I like to imagine the party they were purchased for, the summer vacation where they were excitedly packed in the suitcase, or maybe a job interview when the owner decided to make a change in her life.

When I start a project, I feel a sense of responsibility (oftentimes fear) in making those first cuts. 'Snip snip' – there's no going back – 'stitch stitch'. Things begin to change quickly, and – 'smile smile' – in no time the fear has disappeared and been replaced with a warm, humming glow. It is that creative buzz that draws me into the studio every day. *Oui Oui!* Add a little Parisian romance to your world. This feminine and sexy dress is designed from a 1930s vintage corset, a 1940s cotton-layered petticoat, a vintage silk scarf, the straps from a thrifted silk camisole and a textile cut from a pretty floral dress.

All of the pieces came together to form this one-of-a-kind dress. The sash at the waist is attached and there is a 22 inch zipper (about 55cm) on the side. The petticoat has three layers; the bottom is a lovely white eyelet. An ivory-pleated silk panel creates interest as you walk away.

The skirt is sheer and I would recommend wearing a slip underneath.

Featured on the cover of *Belle Armoire* magazine.

Recycled. One-of-a-kind. Always.

Lori Marsha

Materials

Second-hand stores, jumble sales and hand-me-downs

Corset
Skirts and petticoats
Pretty scarves, chiffon and netting
Scraps of lace, linen, buttons and braid, feathers, beads and trinkets to embellish

Craft supplies

Scissors
Needle and thread

TIP:
How to build a dress from a corset

I find that a bra or a corset can be a great basis to get the ball rolling and create a dress. In fact it provides a real head start. Corsetry is such an art and I have found that starting from scratch to create a corset is a fiddly business – getting a good shape and fit can be a painstaking process. So I tend to pick up a good corset whenever I find one – and have never failed to use it to good advantage.

When I have designed for women with full figures I have found that starting with a well-fitting bra and building the dress onto the bra is a great way of getting a good fit. For the less well-endowed, a good fitting corset can work wonders to create a surprising cleavage!

To make this dress I would first develop the bodice and skirt as separate pieces, then join them together at the waist before fitting the zipper. The sash would be the final touch.

Add a Victorian-looking choker and three-quarter-length gloves for a dramatic evening effect

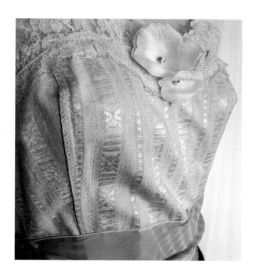

The bodice

1   To transform the corset from a piece of underwear to the bodice of a pretty frock, embellish it with lace, beads, sequins, flowers or even feathers. Lori has used beautiful soft colours and some antique lace to decorate her bodice.

2   An alternative is to use a black corset and go for it with some touches of red in the embellishments to create a raunchier look. Sometimes I use rows of beads and drape them under the bustline, catching them at the centre front. This looks theatrical and fun. I have even added a bead or rosette to suggest the nipple! I like to add a Victorian-looking choker and find that three-quarter-length gloves can really spice things up to create a dramatic evening effect.

The skirt

3   There is so much you can do to create a layered skirt. I suggest that you start by deconstructing old skirts and/or dresses,

play with the pieces and decide which layers you want to include in your skirt. The bottom layer looks great if you use lace or a fabric that resembles a petticoat. (If you have it showing just a couple of inches below the other fabric it looks like the petticoat is just peeping out and is rather charming.)

4   Gather each piece of the skirt individually and get the length of the various levels looking right before joining them together at the top and stitching the entire skirt to the bodice. Even a short skirt can look great with two or three layers in it. If the fabric is quite light, a layered design works well, but if the fabric is heavier there will be too much bulk at the waist and it can look lumpy. This can be avoided by attaching the gathered part of the skirt to a basque – this is shaped like the top of a fitted skirt that is chopped off at the relevant level and the gathered skirt joined to it. This minimises fullness at the waist. Sometimes I like to add a piece of fabric draped over the frills and caught at the waist on either side as this looks a bit like theatre curtains and creates a lush, full effect.

5   If the corset is the kind that extends below the waist I suggest that you sew the skirt to the corset just below the waist. This dropped waist effect is very flattering and creates a slimmer looking waist. A sash can, quite literally, pull it all together! I quite like to keep it separate for maximum flexibility. Or you can fully commit and attach it to the dress as in Lori's romantic creation.

Di Jennings

Antique Bride

‘ Inspired by images from
1920s silent movies, the end
result is oh, so romantic! ’

Antique Bride

THE 'ANTIQUE BRIDE' references the tradition of the 'Hope Chest', in which young girls would amass collections of silks for their wedding and linens for the home in preparation for the rite of passage into married life.

Originally known as 'cassone', these boxes were ornately decorated and heavily gilded, a staple of dynastic marriages in Renaissance Italy. The chest itself was a symbol of wealth and status, a gift to the husband of far greater worth than its contents.

The cassone was traditionally presented at birth, which meant that by the time the girl was of marriageable age (at about twelve years old), the fabrics inside would be laced with holes from heavy moth infestation. The royal seamstress would artfully sew the fabric in layers, creating the kind of diaphanous gown still favoured by many brides across the world today. In fact, even after the advent of moth repellent cedar chests, lace makers continue to imitate this fragile fabric form, despite it being associated with the moth infested days of the Renaissance.

In a bid to rid the dress of its unwanted inhabitants on the big day, the bride would wear bunches of Syrian 'borage' under her skirt. Otherwise known as 'star flower' this blue-petalled herb is well known for its moth-repelling properties; essential for a young bride wishing to avoid the humiliation of moths flying out from under her skirt in the chapel. Hence the old adage: 'Something old, something new, something borrowed and something blue…' – the blue of course referring to a bunch of borage, a superstition which is held up to this day with a simple blue garter.

As the bride and groom left the church, well-wishers would shower them with salts, calling, 'Longevity to the linen of love!'. Before the groom carried the bride over the threshold he would 'hold a torch to her', usually an ornate candelabra which would hopefully draw out the last few moths before they began their new life together.

Kate MacKay

Design

Creating the antique bride was one of the few times that I went shopping for elements to use in a project, rather than just looking around my home and seeing what I already have stashed away. I was initially inspired when I came across a pretty cream-coloured corset in a charity shop. I thought of the acres of old lace doilies and table mats I had seen on my travels and decided to make an antique bride dress.

As it happened, I subsequently found everything I wanted in the first charity shop I came to. There was an abundance of cream and white table runners and pieces of old lace as well as some old pearl jewellery and even some scented cream roses. Perfect! I have decided that I must be on the right track with this work, because everything I need is always at my fingertips.

Di Jennings

Materials

Second-hand stores, jumble sales and hand-me-downs

White linen tablecloth
Old cream table runner
Lace doilies
Cotton embroidered table mats
Old lace shawl
Plastic cream roses
Costume pearl-style beads

Craft supplies

Scissors
Needle and thread
Dressmaker's pins and
safety pins
Tea bags

TIP:

How to work with a mix of different elements

The beauty of working in this way is that rather than coming up with a design at the outset, I play in front of the mirror with the various pieces and the design starts to emerge. In this case, the long table runner was perfect for the train and the square tablecloth looked like it would work well as a skirt.

The only problem was that when I put it all together, the skirt looked too white against the coffees and creams of the other elements. So I made a tea bath to give the cloth an antique sepia look. To do this, place about six tea bags into boiling water and leave to brew. Then soak the white item in the tea bath for a few hours. This will only work with natural fabrics like cotton and silk.

Soak white fabrics in tea
for an antique sepia look

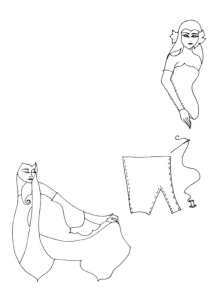

TIP:
How to make decorative sleeves

The sleeves are quite elaborate and made from about ten different pieces of lace. I love the way the embroidered corner of the serviette creates a V-shape onto the hand. Simple elbow-to-wrist coverings are such a good way to complete a bodice-based outfit such as this, they effectively pull all the different parts of the outfit together.

1   Measure the length from your hand to your wrist, then measure the width around your upper arm and wrist.

2   Cut a sleeve shape accordingly in light cotton, like a sheet or pillowcase. Pin carefully onto a willing volunteer's arm, remembering to allow space for the elbow to bend, then seam.

3   Begin to pin and sew your lace elements along your sleeve in a way that complements the line of the garment and makes the most of the pieces that you have gathered. Make features of interesting bits of embroidery and use the ready-made patterned edges to complete the top and cuffs. You can attach a corner to the middle finger with a loop of ribbon to achieve that 'medieval princess' line. Layering lace in slight pleats around the elbow serves to disguise the part of the sleeve that needs a bit of movement.

Di Jennings

An embroidered corner of a serviette makes a great sleeve detail

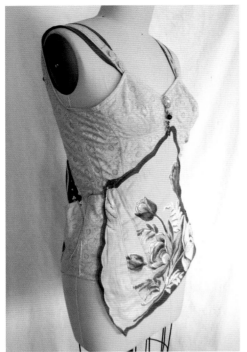

Reworked
Corset

❝The structure of the garment
is there already; all you have
to do is embellish and extend
it to your heart's desire!❞

Reworked Corset

COILED IN WHALEBONE, caged in wire, waists clinched, bosoms heaving, heart beating like a humming bird; the heady pleasures of asphyxiation were well known to Victorian ladies, endured all in the name of fashion. Bemused male doctors searched for a cure to the malady of hysteria that so tragically only befell the young fashionable female elite. 'Fainting rooms' became a must-have of the stylish entertainer, featuring the classic easy-access, supine-recline *chaise longue* couches, perfectly designed for dignified collapse.

Smelling salts were at a premium, an essential accessory for every chivalrous gent likely to overexcite the more easily flustered middle-class maidens. Perturbed professors continued their search for a cure for the malady of the day and careful research at the time noted that hysteria occurred less in corseted women when they were working on their samplers, practicing musical scales and perfecting their floral arrangements.

There was a marked influx in the fainting rooms when women had been drinking coffee, riding horses or reading French novels whilst wearing a corset. The diagnosis was clear: it was sinful to indulge in such activities when corseted, as it opened the channels for the Devil to enter the womb and possess the young lady until she was revived by an upstanding male pillar of society. This condition was swiftly diagnosed by the clever Victorian medical profession as 'womb fury': a madness which ensued from unsatisfied and unbridled carnal desire, prevalent in unmarried women or those with impotent husbands. The insanity of insatiable embracement so envelops the patient, that she would utter wanton and lascivious speeches (see Lazurus Riverius, *The Practice of Physick London* (1655)).

Surprisingly, despite this terrifying diagnosis, corsets continued to become ever more popular, even with men, who could of course indulge in the said activities in their corsets with no fear of experiencing a demon-possessed womb. The enquiring mind might query why men wore the tight corsets at all when they did not achieve the desired male silhouette – and bearing in mind the associated ailments – to which the corseted chap would reply simply that it eased 'back ache' before sipping his café latte and returning to the pages of his French novel.
Kate MacKay

Design

'Passionate, romantic, feminine. Let's not forget sexy.'

The above are just words but they do convey a sense of what this corset top is about. The 100 per cent cotton base piece is incredibly detailed circa the late 1940s or early 1950s with fourteen buttons. Buttons that you will painstakingly fasten in the hope of turning unfastening into a collaborative effort at the end of the evening.

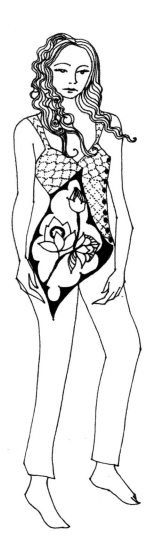

The addition of vintage textiles – soft cotton hankies in lovely floral and ribbon prints – together with a lovely dangling string of vintage buttons and jewellery findings complete what might fittingly be described as a 'romance enabler'.

Spring signals the arrival of *freshness*. As I was hanging a few scraps of laundered lace on the back fence this morning, I took a moment for myself. It was a coolish morning and the sun was shining through wispy cloud-filtered light. I took a deep breath, spied the new leaves on the rose bushes and was thankful again, for my opportunity to create. The day felt promising...

I'm working on a line of romantic spring dresses; dresses that also hold a promise...a promise to allow the wearer to understand and believe in her beauty, to appreciate the tactile sensuality of natural textiles and to create a memory on a special day.

Lori Marsha

TIP:

How to make an empire dress from a camisole

1 To make a pretty empire line dress, cut the camisole top under the bust to make it shorter and sew on a skirt.

2 Try joining old square silk scarves to make the skirt section, scarves often come in romantic floral prints that work well with underwear.

3 Experiment by folding them on the diagonal and pinning them along the bottom of the camisole top. This will create a layered effect with lots of movement and a dynamic alternating hemline.

4 If the dress is to be worn over jeans or hot pants you can attach the scarves soley at the top, allowing them to flow and hang naturally. Otherwise pin and sew the edges together to create a solid fabric.

5 Try to play with layering the scarves; you could have longer ones underneath and shorter ones on top for example. The best way is to pin the items you have collected in a variety of ways using a tailor's dummy if you have one or a willing friend if not. Take account of the weight and hang of the fabric, the colours and patterns and shape of your pieces. Through trial and error you will be able to use these to their best advantage.

6 Alternatively find a nightie that works well with the camisole, cut it just below the bust and join the bottom section to the camisole top.

7 I suggest adding a contrasting sash under the bust to dress it up a little.

Di Jennings

Materials

Second-hand stores and hand-me-downs

Camisole top
Skirt or negligee
Scarves and ribbons

Craft supplies

Scissors
Needle and thread

Vintage scarves often come in romantic floral prints that work well with underwear

Illustrated Dress

‘ I love the way the drawing
adorns the body; images
become animated as the fabric
shifts with each movement ’

Illustrated Dress

THE WITCH HUNTS of the reformation are renowned for their cruel prejudice, horrific trials and twisted reasoning. Women could be accused of witchcraft for little or no reason and once accused, the trial was a sentence in itself. A popular method of trial was to plunge the accused into a lake: if she floated she was a witch and would be burned at the stake, if she drowned she was not a witch and was permitted a Christian burial.

One such unfortunate soul was 'Raven Mary' of Hammersmith in London. Mary had been an educated lady of the court, she was beautiful, literate and her embroideries were unsurpassed. All of this promised a bright future were it not for the witch-hunters. Accused of the dubious crime of feeding ravens, thought to be winged messengers of the Devil, Mary was locked in the Tower of London, where she spent thirteen nights, given nothing but a quill and ink to write her final will and testament. Each night the guard would come for the letter and find Mary sitting in the shadows, the quill inked in anticipation but the page unmarked. On the dawn of the 14th day she was brought before the baying crowd, her silk gown rustling and glowing in the stark light of the morning. It was covered in the finest calligraphy, the most intricate drawings ever seen. Like an illuminated manuscript of walking silk and ink, she silently paraded her last will and testament before the hordes. Legend has it that as the flames licked their way up the silk, birds of smoke, in shadowy silhouettes filled the sky until it was raven black. Today there is a park called Ravenscourt near where she used to live and ravens still flock to the Tower of London, said to be searching for Raven Mary.

Kate MacKay

Design

The Illustrated Dress is my solution to a phobia of following patterns and an inability to work in three dimensions. A simple silk petticoat I picked up on a stall at a music festival and my old faithful permanent marker were all I needed to create this one-off wearable fairytale.

I once saw an exhibition where they had some of the actual garments featured in the paintings of Gustav Klimt alongside the original artwork. Since then I have always wanted to create screen-printed or wood-block printed versions of my illustrations and exhibit them in a similar way. As usual, an aversion to the technical process, equipment and space required put me off. This is an accessible and immediately gratifying alternative which is even nicer in some ways because it is truly unique.

I love the way the drawing adorns the body, particularly with the silk, the images become animated as the light fabric shifts with each movement. The beautiful thing about this project is that it can be so personal; I'd love to do a christening gown with all the hopes for the future drawn on.

Kate MacKay

Materials

Second-hand store

Silk petticoat – or any plain silk garment
(I have subsequently illustrated a silk tie amongst other things)

Your recycling

Collect pictures to trace and embellish (newspapers, magazines, flyers and greetings cards are great sources of inspiration)

Craft supplies

Permanent marker – or use fabric pens for a longer lasting piece
Tracing paper
Photocopier (optional, for those with drawing vertigo)

TIP:
How to design a line drawing

1 Gather together images that catch your eye from magazines, newspapers, greeting cards and flyers, photocopy illustrations you like from books or photos you have taken.

2 Choose a strong, simple image as a starting point. When I was a child my doodles always used to begin with an eye, now it is usually a swallow.

3 Trace this image somewhere on your page, try to forget about what it actually is and enjoy the form, the shape, contrasts of light and dark. When you remove the traced image you can begin to extend and exaggerate elements of the design; develop a hairstyle into a pattern of circles and spirals, a bird's wing into a patchwork of diamonds.

4 Choose another image from your array and slot it into the design under the tracing paper. You may want to trace just an element of this one; half a face to emerge from behind foliage or crashing waves to flow out of a top hat.

5 Keep adding to the design in this way, choosing images that complement each other and echo forms with additional shapes and patterns. Let the drawing sprawl across the page, enjoy the process – you can select the best bits later.

TIP:
How to draw on silk

The nice thing about silk is that if you are not confident with drawing you can trace an image or at least use tracing as a starting point.

1 Place your design on a piece of plain paper, between the layers of the dress; make sure the ink has dried so that it doesn't smudge onto the fabric. I used an ordinary permanent marker pen for this, which can bleed a bit and might not withstand lots of wear. Fabric pens are probably a better bet; I like the ones that are just like marker pens.

2 Start to trace the design onto the fabric, when placing the illustrations think about how the garment will be worn on the body. The way the light fabric hangs from and hugs the figure can really be enhanced by your drawing.

Kate MacKay

Put plain paper between layers of the dress to stop the pen going through to the back

Chapter 2:

Plastic

April Showers

POST-WAR AMERICAN CONSUMPTION was led largely by the wave of fantastic plastics hitting the market. A newly-invigorated sense of carefree optimism and prosperity seemed to be summed up succinctly in this seemingly endless range of colourful, cheap yet durable plastic gimmicks which were to become staple icons of suburban success.

The Mid-West market was largely dominated by Earl Tupper's food-preserving 'Tupperware', due to its clever promotion through networks of housewives hosting 'Tupperware parties'. Formica was also prevalent, providing as it did a durable and attractive easy-wipe surface for any light plywood structure.

In a bid to raise the game, bathroom-furnishing giants Aq-ware launched the travelling 'shower shows'. These were to be the medicine show of a new disposable consumer culture. Show tunes and jingles accompanied demonstrations and displays of all kinds of plastic paraphernalia necessary to furnish and accessorise the dream lagoon of any domestic goddess. Many then revolutionary, now familiar items such as bath pillows, 'his and hers' towels, 'up' and 'down' cloths, toilet roll dresses and sanitary bags (to name but a few) were first launched at these shows.

Of course no shower show was complete without the famous Shower Girl Dance Troupe. These girls would dance, sing and if the setting was right, perform synchronised swimming routines. Their costumes were made from shower curtains displaying the patterning in vogue. These outfits, whilst modest and practical in form, were actually quite risqué in nature, as they were mostly transparent. Perhaps with a playful reference to the not-so-prim goings-on in the privacy beyond the picket fence, the outfits would mimic the twin-sets, garden and loungewear of the day. The example pictured here is a classic two-piece comprising of an A-line raincoat and a Paddington Bear hat, subtly accessorised with a matching red umbrella.

Kate MacKay

Design

I was a 50s child and grew up with some fabulous 50s wallpaper. Our bathroom remains a vivid memory – black wallpaper with brightly-coloured fish swimming around in an iridescent seascape. It made bath time so much fun! When I found this plastic shower curtain I immediately fell for its 1950s appeal. It was just asking to be made into a raincoat… I decided on a simple A-line shape, as working with plastic can be challenging. I suggest you keep your design simple with as few seams as possible.

Di Jennings

Materials

Second-hand stores, jumble sales and hand-me-downs

Plastic shower curtain with bold attractive patterning

Your recycling

Scrap paper

Craft supplies

Needle and thread
Domestic iron

TIP:
How to work with plastic

I prefer to hand stitch when working with plastic. I suggest that you only machine stitch if you have a walking foot (used for stitching leather). Actually I like to hand stitch as much as possible – I find it so much more relaxing than using a sewing machine, especially as it can be done while having a chat, listening to music or watching TV.

The challenge when working with plastic is working out how to press seams open and flat. This was a trial and error process. As all plastics are different I suggest that you experiment on a fabric scrap before you embark on your garment. When working with fabric we normally just press the seams open with the iron, but that is of course a no-no with plastic! A safe method is to make your seam in the normal way, then topstitch on one side only, catching both seams to one side as you stitch.

However, when I was working on the 'April Showers' outfit I discovered that I could use an iron if I placed paper between the iron and the garment. I was very careful about the length of time that I applied the heat. In fact, I found that if I got the time just right the plastic would begin to fuse. Perfect! But there is a fine line between fusing and melting so be very careful. Don't use newspaper as you may find that the newsprint bleeds on to your creation. On the other hand, if it looks good go for it. Some of my most inspirational ideas have been born from mistakes!

TIP:
How to cut a simple pattern… the lazy way…

My pattern-making teacher would be most unimpressed if she saw the way that I work these days. When I learned pattern cutting it was a very exacting business. I always struggled with tailoring and working with exact measurements. I started having fun when I got into more experimental work and played with shape in a looser, more creative way. I often use existing garments that fit well as a template for the basic shape and then play creatively with other shapes for collars, cuffs, frills etc. If you have a dressmaker's dummy it is fun to drape, cut and slash fabric while it is pinned on the dummy to get the right shape. This avoids the paper cutting stage altogether, is good fun and feels very hands on.

But sometimes I like to make a paper pattern and work on a flat surface. I often use newspaper – if the page is not big enough for the pattern piece just tape 2 pages together.

1 For the 'April Showers' raincoat I found a simple A-line dress and used this as the basic shape for my pattern.

2 Getting armholes and tops of sleeves the right shape can be challenging. Mark with a pencil around the shape of the garment at the seamlines – and remember to add a seam allowance before cutting out the paper pattern.

3 I like to keep different scissors for paper and fabric as cutting paper blunts a good pair of dressmaker's scissors. When I cut the fabric from the pattern I cut the centre back along the fold of the fabric and the centre front along the selvedges, leaving a few centimetres for an overlap and folding back front edges where the coat is fastened.
Di Jennings

Use paper between the
iron and garment when
pressing plastic

Spiral Brooches

❝ Mundane material is magically transformed in these brooches made from plastic bags ❞

Spiral Brooches

THE WET GREY COBBLES of Edinburgh's Royal Mile are beset on both sides by the alluring lights of the colourful shops. Jars of whisky, pewter pots and polished kilt pins, tacky postcards, sickly sweets, embellished hip flasks and foreign newspapers are hung, stacked and piled in every possible nook and cranny. Teetering together like tipsy old friends, the windowpanes and doorways jostle for the attention of the curious passer-by. These old shops remember the centuries, the trinkets and treasures their bellies have held. The tiniest shops – that you'd miss if a seagull or juggler were to catch your eye for less than an instant – were called the 'locking booths', home of the ancient Luckenbooth brooch. These tiny heart-shaped brooches with silver crowns were worn by young lassies as a rite of passage and a protective charm. Bold Scottish lads would give these silver symbols to their 'dillys' (or sweethearts) as a gesture of betrothal; it also signified the maiden's passage into womanhood and was thought to protect the wearer from the evil eye. The Luckenbooth brooch was a considerate present indeed from a prospective partner, with properties that endured far beyond the first flush of romance.

Aside from being a romantic gesture or an attractive way to pin your plaid, if placed under the blouse and close to her heart the Luckenbooth would ease the pain of childbirth, if attached to the petticoat beside the left thigh it ensured a good flow of breast milk and finally pinned to the young bairn's shawl, it protected the wean from being stolen by fairies. Over the years the crafters of the jewellery quarter in Edinburgh have developed and embellished the original little heart, it has matured into two ornate hearts linked together with fine silver knot work, studded with garnets and engraved with calligraphy. However, the true value of the Luckenbooth lies in the essence of its story and the intent with which it is offered: as a tiny charm that is lucky in love, displays a heart that is consistent and symbolises a deep and enduring friendship.

Kate MacKay

Design

The creations I produce include knitted textiles and jewellery in a wide variety of forms. Each piece is unique due to the materials I source and each carries its own history of elements – which could be incorporating a painted glass button from the 1950s or a remnant of fabric from a vintage skirt.

Inspiration arrives in a wide variety of ways. The colours, shapes and textures in the Scottish environment and the raw materials I find provide a seemingly endless source of stimulation that triggers my ideas.

I am interested in 1920s and 30s geometric patterns, colours, fashion illustrations and posters and these influence my textile designs as I enjoy the muted yet vibrant colour combinations. Ideas emerge and are informed from experiences and from a constant exposure to new things and places.
Sarah Galliers

TIP:
How to make a spiral brooch

I like to try and find a use for materials that cannot be recycled. For these jolly spiral brooches I was inspired by my own coiled raffia table mats. I was keen to add brooches to my collection of recycled jewellery. I experimented using orange nets but have found the best results are achieved by using plastic bread bags or Sunday supplement magazine plastic mail bags which are soft and pliable.

1   Cut long strips of plastic, about 2 inches (roughly 5 cm) wide.

2   Coil soft wire along the length of the strip.

3   Start bending one end of the strip into a coil shape and secure with small stitches using coloured cotton thread adding seed beads as you progress round (try to keep the coil tight as you go). Allow the stitching to become part of the design by using a complementary colour of thread, it will look like a delicate spider's web covered in dew.

4   Once the complete spiral shape is achieved you can tuck the end of the plastic bags in at the back, or make a feature of the material by making them into tassels that hang decoratively. Sometimes I think it is fun to give a little hint of the mundane material that has been magically transformed – it's all part of the intrigue of the item! Once you are happy with the shape and embellishment, stitch on a metal brooch back. Add extra beads, sequins or a central button if desired.

Sarah Galliers

Materials

Your recycling

Soft plastic from bread bags or magazine wrapping

Second-hand stores, jumble sales and hand-me-downs

Buttons and beads
Brooch pin

Craft supplies

Thin coil of soft wire or copper
Needle and thread

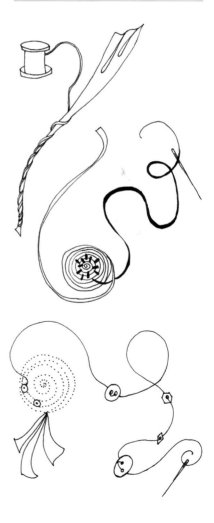

Summer
Collection

‘White supermarket bags with coloured logos make a lovely speckled hat and bag set ’

Summer Collection

SINCE THE 1950s a circular course of wind and currents have been drawing urban flotsam and jetsam out into the pacific where it is spun on the ocean's spool into a spiralling blanket of trash. The trappings of a blindly optimistic disposable age are knitted together to form the island's foundation. This is the land to which the out-of-sight and out-of-mind migrate, the influx of her immortal plastic settlers accelerating for half a decade. 'The Great Pacific Garbage Patch', as she is known, grows in girth relative to consumer consumption. Her increasingly obese mass of rancid plastics currently weighs in at 3.92 million US tonnes (355.6 million kg) and sprawls at least 1,500 miles (3885 km) wide; a giant abiding effigy to man's faith in the infinite.

The devout capitalist can make the pilgrimage to the Mecca-of-his-making in style. From the comfort of his cruise ship he can gaze through rose-tinted Ray-Bans and witness the miracle of man residing over nature. Whilst marinating his torso in coconut oil, he can observe the great and mighty ocean and all the birds and beasts that live within submit to the collective poisonous power of the human's humble plastic bottle, testament indeed to the power of the mass. If he chooses to take a trip to shore, man can take the time to revel in the mine of recent memory; he might titter in delight at the mobile phone of yesterday or even shed a nostalgic tear at his old space-hopper bobbing in the breeze. He can sample local crafts, textiles and traditional dress woven from these repugnant reeds. Before sailing home, he can load up his bespoke matching luggage set with souvenirs for his wife and kids; a stylish sun hat or a novelty purse, he is welcome to take as much as he likes because this crop really is infinite. No force of nature or even man himself can ever move this Olympian bin, the sun sets, Neptune kneels and man finally is immortal.

Kate MacKay

Design

This collection of hats and bags made from white plastic bags represents the beginning of my creative plastic bag adventures. I had just arrived in Edinburgh, was missing my friends back home in New Zealand and I needed something to keep me occupied while I developed a social life, so I started playing with plastic in those long, lonely evenings. As it happened this work was the catalyst to connect with Kate and the wonderful group of artists that she works with as part of Alchemy Arts.

This is how it happened. I was sitting in a café, feeling rather flash sporting my new hat and bag. A charming young woman at the next table reached over to look at the bag and asked, 'Is that made from plastic bags?' and we started chatting. This was the beginning of a great friendship and working relationship with Kate. Within a month we were working together on a community arts project, bouncing creative ideas off of each other... and the seed of this book was sown.

Working with white was a change for me as I generally work with strong colours (in fact none of these bags are pure white as most of the bags I had collected had a coloured logo, and this created a speckled effect that I rather liked). The use of white, red and blue Tesco supermarket's carrier bags prompted quite a nautical look in a couple of the pieces. The process was mainly intuitive and the ideas emerged as I worked. Sometimes I like to just let my fingers do the talking and allow my busy mind to be quiet. I find this way of working to be therapeutic and quite meditative. With each of the pieces I started by making shapes – circles, rectangles etc. – and the designs emerged as I went along. The process was helped by the addition of recycled belts added here and there for decoration or to fasten the bag.

Di Jennings

Materials

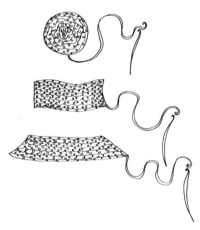

TIP:

How to make a black and white bowler hat

This was the first hat I made and remains a firm favourite. I wear it a lot and it is much admired. I like the fact that I can throw it into a bag or suitcase and it just bounces back into shape. The hat is crocheted. When I cut the plastic I made the width of the plastic 'ribbon' about ⅓ inch (1cm) – this made the work quite chunky. And of course the chunkier the plastic, the quicker the hat takes shape.

1   I started by making a circle of chain stitches and worked rows of trebles to form a circle to make the top of the hat.

2   To make the side section, I cast on about 10 chain stitches and worked rows of trebles to make a strip long enough to equal the circumference of the circular piece. Then I stitched the short ends of the long strip together, and hand sewed it to the outer edge of the circle to form a pillbox shape.

3   Then I crocheted the brim. I cast on enough stitches to equal the circumference of the pillbox. Then I worked rows of trebles to create a brim about 3 inches (8cm) wide. To create a good brim shape, I reduced the number of stitches in the last 3 rows. This helped the brim to turn upward – or it can be turned down, depending on the look you want. It is quite a versatile hat.

4   The final touch is the addition of a hat band that is cut from a black and white woven belt I had collected on my jumble sale travels.

TIP:
How to make a bucket bag

1 I found several rolls of red and white plastic tape in a scrap store. I think it was initially intended to be used by police to mark off a crime scene! 'Hooray', I thought – this would bypass the time-consuming business of cutting up plastic bags. The plastic ribbon was quite chunky so I decided to knit this bag, rather than crochet, using large knitting needles. The red and white diagonal stripes knitted up to create an attractive dappled pattern. The knitting grew pretty fast, but I needed regular shakes of talcum powder to stop the work from sticking.

2 The bag is a very simple design and is made of a long rectangle (twice the length of the bag) that is sewn at the sides.

3 The handles are made from lengths of canvas tape.

4 Down the centre of the bag I have hand sewn two rows of embroidered, mirrored braid (cut from an old blouse that was past its 'use-by' date).

5 A narrow blue patent belt is attached to the opening to finish the edge.

When using plastic tape, sprinkle your work with talc to stop it sticking

TIP:
How to make a pom-pom hat

1 To make the pom-pom hat, I started by making a small pill box shape as above and hand stitched a length of beaded ribbon to the edge.

2 For the large flower-like decoration on the side I used about 20 chain stitches and worked several rows of trebles. I increased the number of trebles in each row to create a flared effect, and then decreased the number of trebles in the last couple of rows. This made the 'flower' fold back at the edges like a petal. After casting off, I joined the short ends and gathered up the inner circle to create a flower shape. I sewed this to the side of the hat, then to create a centre for the flower added a fluffy red pom-pom that had fallen off an old scarf.

Di Jennings

Hula!

Hula!

THE ECO-CONSCIOUS STREET-COMBER swaps flora for flotsam, at once a fashionable solution to marine pollution and a godsend for hay fever sufferers everywhere. As anyone who has ever been plagued by an acute pollen allergy knows only too well, the traditional Pacific *lei* could be nothing short of deadly. What to some may be a floricultural fantasy of light and colour to others may be a perennial pain darkened by the threat of anaphylaxis. The dangers of an unexpected allergic reaction haunt us all.

These garlands, gaudy as a hothouse, are durable and plentiful. To those who can see that disposable goods and imperishable goods are often the same, the high street becomes a haven, abundant in these bin-bag blossoms. Our shopping bag *lei* celebrates the exotic in the everyday, supermarket drudgery yields an urban pacific princess. A shoal of synthetics threaded bumper to bumper, this is the spaghetti junction of the South Sea Isles.

Worn as a headdress or necklace, the idea behind the *lei* is that it can be made out of anything and used to celebrate any occasion, but it must always be given with love and must never be thrown away or discarded. Be it plastic, paper, bones or seeds, when it falls into disuse it should be returned to the elements from which it came, or transformed into another decoration – in true Alchemy Arts style.

Kate MacKay

Design

I have lived in New Zealand for much of my life and have always adored Pacific Island style. It is so colourful and conjures up aromas of frangipani and coconut alongside images of long leisurely summer days spent sipping exotic fruity cocktails to the sounds of the ukulele, as warm waves break gently onto a palm fringed beach. Paradise! Our beautiful 'Hula Girl' outfit is made from shredded Sainsbury's supermarket plastic carrier bags, woven place mats and fake flowers. The *lei* headdress features flowers and leaves that have been crocheted from brightly coloured plastic shopping bags.

Di Jennings

Materials

Your recycling

Brightly coloured plastic bags
Egg boxes

Second-hand stores, jumble sales and hand-me-downs

Bright woven place mats
Plastic flowers

Craft supplies

Needle and thread
Knitting needle
Crochet hook
Pins

There will be some trial and error involved; that is part of the fun. Your flower will be truly unique!

TIP:

How to make a flower from a plastic bag

1 Select a range of plastic shopping bags in hot, tropical colours. Cut the first plastic bag so that it is open at both ends. Start at one end and cut with sharp scissors in a diagonal direction around the circumference of the bag. When you have completed the first round, widen out slightly so that you form a continuous strand of plastic about ½ inch (1 ½cm) wide. The narrower you cut, the finer the work will be; conversely, the wider the plastic 'ribbon' you create as you cut, the sturdier your end result will be.

2 When you have finished cutting, roll the plastic ribbon into a ball. You are now ready to start crocheting (or knitting – use the skill that you are most familiar with). I chose to experiment with crochet. Each of my flowers is slightly different – there is no 'right way' but start with a few chain stitches that form a circle and make that the centre of the flower. As you add rows of crochet (I started with treble stitches) fashion it in such a way that it takes the shape of a flower.

3 For the centre of the flower there are many options: a spare bead or a large sequin...or if embroidery is your thing, embroider a large French knot into the middle of the flower. I crocheted a hibiscus-looking stem from a firm ribbon and knotted it at the end. Make several flowers and if you are feeling ambitious try your hand at a leaf or two. Arrange and stitch them onto a headband (I made mine from, you guessed it, crocheted shopping bags!).

TIP:
How to make *lei* from hazard tape

The important thing is to wait until the hazard is over before you reclaim the tape! We often get reams of this after we have taken part in a festival or public event, where it has been used to mark out temporary car parks and the like. Any light plastic cut into strips will do though, like the sort used to make bin bags or disposable tablecloths.

1 Cut a piece of string at the length you want (this style of *lei* works well for ankles and wrists).

2 Tie a knot in one end and tape the other end to a double-ended knitting needle.

3 Begin to concertina the plastic strip by folding it backwards and forwards. Thread this onto the knitting needle.

4 Keep on like this, threading and folding until the needle is full, then start to push the concertina onto the string. When the string is full, tie the ends together with a knot. This simple technique can look really great with a variety of coloured plastic, or you can thread buttons and beads in between plastic sections.

TIP:
How to make *lei* from egg boxes

Whilst the thought of making something from egg boxes may prompt you to recall fiascos from kindergarten, Pacific women show just how beautifully this everyday material can be transformed.

1 Simply cut the box into individual cups then cut the edges into zig-zags.

2 Paint the cups in bright contrasting colours and thread them onto a string. Elastic thread is strong and flexible, but anything will do really.

3 Measure your headdress to rest elegantly on your head and secure with a knot, simple!

Di Jennings

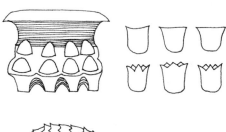

Toy Jewellery

‘ Fun flotsam and jetsam
jewellery: nostalgia salvaged
from childhood to bring joy
to grown-ups ’

Toy Jewellery

LEGEND HAS IT that St Kitts was the golden-haired child-king of the North Lands; orphaned on the dark eve of his 8th birthday he was to be crowned king with the rising dawn. And so, the royal nurse began to strip his room of all the trappings of childhood in order to make his chamber fit for the mature mindset of a monarch. Silent tears rolled down Kitts's cheeks as he witnessed his beloved toys being torn from him so prematurely and thrown into the moat. As the nurse continued with the seemingly endless task (he had been quite spoilt) Kitts sat on his throne sobbing and waiting for the dawn.

Spinning tops, skipping ropes and skittles flew out the windows but the dawn did not rise. Board games, playing cards and bouncy balls fell from the turrets yet the dawn still did not rise. Teddy bears, dolls, an Etch-a-Sketch, rubber ducks, model planes and kites all sank into the castle moat and it seemed the eternal night would never end. After a month of darkness, the Royal Nurse collapsed in exhaustion, all the toys gone save a single box of tin soldiers.

It is said that she awoke to a great commotion in the castle grounds; Kitts was sitting on his throne, beaming for the first time in a month, a silver crown glistened atop his golden curls, made entirely of his beloved tin soldiers. The sky that had been black for so long was ablaze with shimmering curtains of colour. People rejoiced at the miracle, declaring that it was an act of God. Kitts solemnly declared that no toy should ever be discarded, and where possible, should instead be fashioned into a wearable memento of the past. St Kitts is now known as the patron saint of lost toys and on St Kitts's Day people parade around town adorned in their favourite childhood relics.

Kate MacKay

Design

Fun flotsam and jetsam jewellery: nostalgia salvaged from childhood adapted to bring joy to grown-ups. These bite-sized projects are wonderfully satisfying to complete. Make a feature of your favourite trinket, pairing it with beads found/ rescued from old necklaces. It's the ultimate in recycled 'statement' neckwear: tongue-in-cheek contemporary pieces made from vintage finds.

Old board game pieces, 'Sindy' doll accessories, Lego, Spirographs, plectrums, even Christmas cracker contents (the cheaper the better) have all yielded results. Nothing is safe from my bejewelling clutches! Scour toy buckets at car boot sales/charity shops or raid your family's attic. Ebay is an option but spoils the spontaneity of happenstance finds.

Maybe it all started with the beloved childhood build-your-own Lego jewellery kit my father brought me back from a business trip (which I still have, wear and love in its remade guise)… Or maybe it started with a fondness for bright colours (as a child I used to only paint in yellow)… But it is more likely that my love of toy-jewellery emerged as the logical conclusion to decades of collecting old toys/ trinkets and obsessive accessorising.

At markets, I always look out for unusual beads or existing necklaces which can be dismantled to complement larger focal pieces. Children's crafty creations can be inspiring for their unselfconscious combining of random colours.
Knitty Kitty

Materials

Second-hand stores, jumble sales and hand-me-downs

Large/mid-sized trinkets
An unwanted necklace or range of beads in colours compatible with your 'key' piece(s)

Craft supplies

Drill and small drill bit
(2mm or ¹⁄₁₆ inch)
Pliers
Craft scissors

Jewellery findings
(not all will be necessary)

Jump/split ring, tiger tail/beading wire, clasp (any type: trigger/ magnetic/toggle) and crimps. Alternatively a length of elastic which you can simply knot to secure (ensure elastic is not too thick to thread through your beads/drilled holes)
– all available from your local craft shop

Optional

soldering iron and flux

TIP:
How to make a toy necklace

In this instance I am using my Super Mario necklace as an example which uses red and dice beads (pre-drilled), assorted Lego shapes, as well as keys from an old editing keyboard to accompany the 'main man'!

1   Decide on a colour range or a theme for the piece.

2   Super Mario himself was originally a key ring and so came pre-drilled, ready for action. Otherwise, drill a small hole in your chosen item. Bear in mind the weight of the object if it is not of a uniform shape – drilling a hole which will allow it to sit flat and evenly. In the case of Mario, the hole drilled was from front to back to enable me to use a ring to hang him from.

3   Next, select a suitable size of jump ring (with a large enough diameter to fit through the hole with room to thread your wire/elastic through).

4   Using pliers, open the jump ring up enough to thread the drilled item through. When doing this, try to make as little alteration to the natural shape of the ring as possible as changing it creates more work as you will want to try and return it to its original shape on closing.

5   If your item is particularly precious, you may wish to secure the jump ring by soldering it. This will prevent the ring from coming apart and your hard work being lost in the street to some other magpie's joy.

6   Alternatively, use a split (instead of 'jump') ring – a small version of the ring used to hold keys and fobs together.

7   In the instance of the Super Mario necklace, I also drilled holes in assorted Lego pieces and keys retrieved from a broken editing keyboard (being a technician by day has untold advantages). This entailed drilling a hole from one side to another. I figured this would sit better than suspending them from rings. Whether you chose this method or the use of a jump/split ring depends on the shape of the item – simple squares such as Lego or keys lie better when flat.

8 Once you have drilled/hung your pieces, the fun begins! Arrange the pieces as you wish and thread them onto your chosen material. In this case, I used red 'Soft Flex beading wire' (test strength is 26lbs – about 1kg 200g) – although the finished item comes nowhere close to that). Ensure the necklace reaches the desired length: many a project has been stalled by only having enough beads to create a circulation-stopping choker! Some pieces, particularly chunkier ones, do not suffer from a plain, wire-exposing back.

9 The ends are secured by threading the end of the wire first through a crimp and then one half of the clasp. Double the thread *back* though the crimp and press down with pliers. Trim the excess length of wire, ensuring it doesn't leave a sharp end which could catch the back of your neck. Repeat for the other side, ensuring you are happy with the order and the fit (there's no going back after you close the second crimp).

Don't underestimate the wonders of a cure-all dollop of glue

Take great pride in having created something utterly unique!

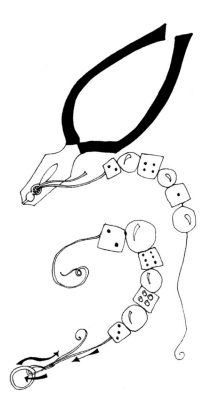

In the Swim

‘An outfit from a combination
of unlikely elements including
retro swimsuit, plastic bag and
discarded umbrella ,

In the Swim

THIS OUTFIT CONSISTS OF CURVES AND CIRCLES, conveying a cheerful buoyancy unique to the kind of poolside attire worn by those who know it's good to get wet. The knitted plastic hat is a defiant nod to the infamous hand knitted woollen swimwear of the 1950s; swimwear that bore a generation haunted by the material's ability to double in length, retain water and sand and remain always itchy yet never dry.

'In the Swim' is an ergonomic yet elegant ensemble. Soft pastels impress lightness overall whilst tough plastics ensure this hourglass silhouette won't turn with the tide. Like all good poolside pin-ups, the figure is modestly revealed and structurally enhanced and the hips are adorned with flirty skirting, which serves to balance the highbrow, cubist motif of the print. It is, to my eye, such oppositions that create the tension in this piece. Does anything say 'holiday' less than a broken brolly discarded in frustration on a windy day? Yet it is exactly such metropolitan flotsam that bridges the gap between 'stylish urban-dweller' and 'creature from the blue lagoon'.

Kate MacKay

Design

This fun outfit includes a combination of unlikely elements including a retro swimsuit, cut off leggings, an overskirt fashioned from a belt and a discarded umbrella, as well as a hat made from crocheted plastic bags. Retro swimsuits are superb – as I have become older, I much prefer them to modern swimsuits. They often have wonderful colours and patterns and the designs are more flattering on less than nubile bodies, but still create a unique sense of style.

The hat that is crocheted from plastic bags was the inspiration for the rest of the outfit. It looked just like a 1920s swimming cap. Actually, the hat would not be too effective in the water, but we couldn't resist using it for the photograph as it looked so great. I initially made the hat for the Scottish winter and lined it with knit fabric to keep cosy and warm…and the plastic keeps some of the rain out!

I like making my outfits so that the pieces can be worn separately where possible to make them versatile. The 'umbrella skirt' is a good example.
Di Jennings

Materials: overskirt

Second-hand stores, jumble sales and hand-me-downs

Discarded umbrella
Woven belt

Craft supplies

Scissors
Needle and thread

Materials: crochet hat

Your recycling

15 plastic bags
Knit fabric scraps
Decorative bits 'n' bobs
(as desired)

Craft supplies

Crochet hook
Needle and thread

TIP:
How to make the umbrella overskirt

Keep your eyes peeled for an old belt and umbrella in the colours you like. I have a fascination with anything woven and collect woven belts from charity shops. I find that a woven belt is very flexible and the woven strands make it easy to attach other elements to it.

I found the umbrella at the Alchemy Arts scrap store. Kate had already used it for a community workshop and it was covered in her delicious-looking drawings. This made it doubly precious: recycling the recycling!

1 First I removed the plastic cover from the umbrella framework and cut a circle in the middle for the waist. As I wanted some gathering at the waist, I made the measurement of the circle at least one-and-a-half times the waist measurement. The bigger the measurement the more gathers you will create.

2 I cut the remainder of the umbrella into 2 circles and made the outer circle around 2 inches (5cm) wider than the inner, smaller circle to create a layered effect on the overskirt.

3 Then I hand gathered each circle of plastic separately so that the waist measurement of each frill equalled the waist measurement. I joined the two frills together to make the wee skirt and then stitched the skirt to the underside of the belt. So cute!

4 I also made a rosette from the piece that was left over from the centre of the umbrella and sewed it to the centre back at the waist. Why waste a scrap when it can be put to good use?

TIP:

How to make a crochet hat

1 I collected plastic bags in shades of blue and green and worked them into balls of 'wool' as described in 'Hula'.

2 I started the hat by making a small circle from chain stitches, then worked a circle of treble stitches into the centre. I kept working rows of trebles and shaped the emerging hat as needed to create a simple bowl shape that hugs the head. This was a trial and error process and involved missing a treble every few stitches. I changed colours every two rows and liked this effect.

3 Once I had a bowl shape that fitted the hat, I tried it on and marked the points where the hat met the front of each ear. I worked several more rows of trebles across the back of the hat leaving the front open for the face.

4 Once the basic shape was complete, I cut lining from some knit fabric scraps using the hat as a template to get the shape right. I hand stitched the lining to the hat.

5 To secure the hat, I then crocheted a strap about ¾ inch (2cm) wide using rows of treble stitches and hand sewed the strap to one side.

6 I made a 'button' by working rows of crochet into a wee ball and sewed it to the other side for fastening. Alternatively, you could use a spare button.

7 The final touch is a leftover piece of braid stitched across the front and a drop bead that came from an old beaded curtain, placed at the centre on the front.

I used plastic bags in complementary colours, but the hat would also look great using black and white bags for an Op art look. Or you could use the colours of your favourite football team – the possibilities are endless…

Di Jennings

Try black-and-white bags for an Op art look

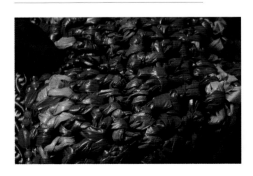

Chapter 3:

Rags and Remnants

'Reconstruct bored and rejected clothing into a contemporary version of a Mayan blouse'

Way Out Huipils

HUIPILS ARE BLOUSES OF MAYAN ORIGIN. They are basically a square or rectangular piece of woven fabric with a hole cut out in the middle for the head and the sides partially sewn together leaving enough space for armholes. Originally, *huipils* were woven on back-strap looms; portable looms that women could carry around with them and thus be able to weave just about anywhere, including in the market square whilst waiting to sell their goods.

The Mayans believed that clothing could transform a person just as a person could transform clothing, the two existing in symbiosis. Because of this magical relationship, Mayans gave their clothing particular significance, dressing, in part, for the gods, believing that the textiles they wore could enhance their religious powers. An infinite number of supernatural symbols were used to appease the gods. Each community had their own designs and motifs for their *huipils*.

But the most interesting aspect of the *huipil* is its cosmic significance. Having the head placed in the very centre of the fabric has specific implications. When a woman places a *huipil* over her head, she enters a symbolic universe. As she sticks her head through the hole, she emerges into the external world and her body becomes the axis of the universe. She is the centre of the world connecting the earth and the sky.

Huipils are narrative. Their symbols and technique indicate religious belief, social background and marital status. Even though the *huipil* has a standard form, the way in which it's embellished makes it unique.

Although for many years the traditional *huipil* was abandoned for more westernized clothing, they have since made a definite comeback. Frida Kahlo instigated their revival. They are also often worn by Mexican folk singer Lila Downs. So why not reconstruct some bored and rejected clothing to make some 'way out' *huipils*?

Cynthia Korzekwa

Design

It's easy to wind up with a collection of tattered T-shirts that are torn, stained or simply unflattering. But these T-shirts can be transformed into 'Way Out *Huipils*', a contemporary version of the traditional Mayan blouse.

In terms of its construction, a *huipil* is basically a rectangular piece of fabric with a hole cut in the centre that's then folded in half. The sides are sewn up leaving openings for the arms. To transform a T-shirt into a *huipil*, you simply cut off the sleeves and side seams to create the centre panel of your *huipil*. Then sew some fabric scraps and old clothing together to create the side panels and sandwich the T-shirt in-between.

Cynthia Korzekwa

Materials

Second-hand stores, jumble sales and hand-me-downs

An old T-shirt
Various scraps of fabric in complementary colours and patterns

Craft supplies

Embroidery thread
Needle and thread
Fabric scissors
Dressmaker's pins

TIP:
How to make a *huipil*

1 To make a *huipil* from a T-shirt, take a ruler and chalk and draw cutting lines. You want to cut the sleeves and side seams off. You will also need to cut off the bottom part of the T-shirt. The amount you cut off depends upon the length of the T-shirt and on your height.

2 Sew your fabric scraps together to create panels that will serve as the borders of your *huipil*. The length of these panels will be the length of the T-shirt's sides (front and back). The width will depend upon the size of the T-shirt and your own size. The example here is around 10 inches (25cm) in width. You can use just about any kind of fabric including old sheets, tea towels and abandoned clothing. You will also need to make panels for the bottom of the front and back of the *huipil*. The width is that of the two side panels plus the bottom of the T-shirt. The length depends upon your height and just where exactly you want the *huipil* to fall.

3 Once all the panels are made, you can sew them together. Do the sides first, then the bottom panels.

4 Once all the panels are attached, you need to sew up the sides leaving openings for the arms (about 10 inches or 25cm). Allow at least ¾ inch (2cm) for seam allowances because you will use it for hemming the sleeve.

5 T-shirt necks are generally not very flattering. So to create a V-neck, turn the *huipil* inside out and with a piece of chalk mark the centre and the length of the opening that you want to make. Cut open, pin back, trim off the excess and sew into place.

6 Hem the *huipil*. The *huipil* is now finished.

Sometimes daily life can distract us and take us in a direction where we hadn't intended to go. So why not embroider a word or a phrase on your *huipil* that represents a personal philosophy to keep you from getting sidetracked? What we wear reflects who we are. So let your intentions be known.

Cynthia Korzekwa

Why not embroider a word or a phrase on your huipil that represents a personal philosophy?

Scarf Wear

❝When working with scarves it is the ornate and complex patterns that get me going❞

Scarf Wear

THE YOUTH OF TODAY may look on in bemusement at the top hat wearing, hanky flailing, bell-adorned, stick-wielding troupe of Middle English men. In these cynical times the sight of snow-white cotton clad bodies skipping and leaping as one impeccably co-ordinated mass might provoke mockery, but if the youth of today were to look closely they would see that the Morris Dancing Man is in fact the break-dancer of a bygone age. The Hertfordshire Hop is his headspin, the village green is his Bronx. Though his street may be decked with bunting rather than graffiti and his beat-box is but the hollow clash of stick against stick, to witness the precision and dexterity of a correctly executed Cotswold Cross would draw appreciative gasps from the most daring street dancer.

However, this is not the fist time Morris Dancing has teetered on the brink of erasure. At the beginning of the 20th century the dance would have gone the way of the dodo, were it not for Mary Neal and the Esperance Club. This was a dressmaking club and co-operative for young working women in London and looking for new dances to perform they chanced upon the Morris. Could it be that, poised at the dawn of a new century we are about to experience another such bold resurgence? I know that the Morris Ring questions the legitimacy and propriety of females dancing the prestigious jig, but if they would look to the streets for their solution this rigorous rite of spring might just survive if not positively blossom. The crisp white cotton squares of cloth waved by the Morris Man today may as well be a flag of surrender if he won't leap into the 21st century with all the boldness of the Abbotts Bromly Horn Dance.

The same white cloths are literally a blank canvas to the Urban All-Girl Morris Troupe. No boil wash glorified boiler suit for her, no blackened face or jingly knees. She is adorned instead in the colourful silk flags that scatter the city's flea markets and car boot sales. Paisley pattern! Pacific print! Provincial polka dot! All stitched together in a patchwork of diversity reflecting the heart of the female city dweller. Her step might be as light and graceful as the silk scarves that adorn her, but like their colourful patterning she is bold and enduring. Just take a look at her at Whitsun, as she dances all the way from London to Norwich, spinning and weaving in colourful flashes of brilliance, like a jigging human May pole.
Kate MacKay

Design

I was first inspired to use scarves to create garments when I saw a dress my friend made for her three-year-old using two contrasting paisley scarves. I love mixing the combinations of colours and pattern. Often the scarves are worn and I have to cut and patch them. If there is a tiny hole I will use beads or sequins to disguise it. I also patch together the left over scraps to make long thin scarves. Nothing is wasted! I find patching and recycling the scarves very satisfying… especially being able to salvage scarves that are threadbare in parts.

All sorts of things inspire me, sometimes it's the fabric itself and sometimes it's an idea that I have and then I source the fabric. When working with scarves it is the ornate and complex patterns that get me going. I love the framing of Persian miniatures and enjoy framing the main 'picture' with contrasting coloured and patterned borders. I find that I need a large collection of scarves to find the right combinations of colour and patterns to create the garments. The scale of the pattern is very important as are the colour combinations.

Kerrie Hughes

Materials

Second–hand stores, jumble sales and hand-me-downs

A range of light silky scarves in complementary colours and designs

Craft supplies

Sewing machine or needle and thread
Dressmaker's pins
Fabric scissors

TIP:

How to make a wraparound skirt from four square scarves

I usually make a wraparound skirt as it fits most people. First I select three scarves that work well together in terms of their colour and patterning. I have made a few of these skirts and through a process of trial and error I have developed the following method. Choose 4 scarves that complement one another. I have called the 4 scarves A, B, C and D. Scarf A will be the most visible, so make scarf A your favourite!

1 First sew scarf A to scarf B along one edge. On scarf A measure a point 10½ inches (27cm) from the bottom edge and 6⅓ inch (16cm) from the right hand corner. Now draw a shallow curve as shown in the diagram and cut along this line. This will form the waistline.

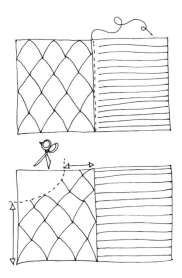

2 On scarf B, draw a line 18½ inches (47 cm) from the edge and parallel to the seam and cut along this line. Now fold scarf C in half and cut along the fold. Sew the pieces back together along short edges to form a long narrow piece and then join the long edge to the bottom of scarves A and B to create the hem. To shape the hem, draw a curve at the bottom of scarf C and cut as per diagram.

3 Finally join scarf D (this will be the under lap) to the side seam of scarf B as shown.

4 To make the waistband, cut a long strip about 3 inches (8 cm) wide from your leftover pieces and attach to the top edge leaving lengths at either end for tying.

5 Finally turn under the hem and stitch in place. This design will create an a-symmetrical look – if you want a more even look you can level the hem.

Kerrie Hughes

When choosing scarves to go together, consider the scale of patterns as well as colour combinations

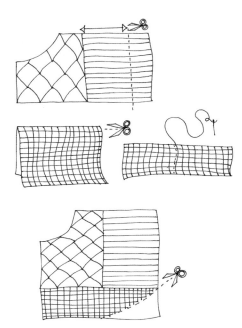

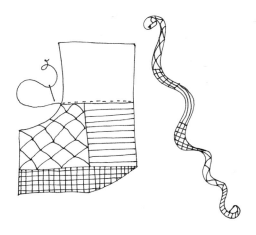

Bedspread
Bags

'A lining rescued from a superhero duvet cover makes this tweed bag both sophisticated and hip'

Bedspread Bags

TO LOOK ATTRACTIVE, INDIVIDUAL AND CONTEMPORARY for the British school attendee is an art of daring and ingenuity. The pallet of school uniforms is a minimal and murky spectrum, ranging from pillar box red through bottle green ending abruptly at navy blue. Like fledgling lawyers, school pupils scour the school rulebook for loopholes, the tighter the restrictions the more powerfully expressive each detail becomes. A single bead threaded onto the lace of a black polished shoe screams 'hippy' stronger than the most garish Kaftan, the impression of a sovereign ring (or 'sovvie') on a gold chain seen under the shirt is a bellowing warning that a girl has a tough boyfriend. With each innovation inching towards individual aestheticism, comes a new school term and the rulebook is revised to quash the rebellion.

An area of amnesty tossed like a bone to style-starved teens is the school bag or satchel. This is the accessory that is without jurisdiction, the catwalk on which to parade your charisma, a constantly-turning and ever-changing fashion wheel.

When I was at school it was the rucksack; sleek and black with flashes of glorious neon. Key-rings, knick-knacks and fluorescent-haired trolls hung from every zip and appendage until it looked like a tinker's cart. The more 'all-terrain' the bag the better; but you should never wear both straps at once or the whole venture would be in vain. Many-the-assembly in which the teachers warned of back problems in later life from this style of carriage, but this and the fear of being dubbed 'an exchange student' only served to strengthen our resolve to dangle these book-laden bags from a lopsided scapular.

Next came the giant sports bag, our books would rattle around in a space designed for a full cricket kit as we ran for the bus, like our own little caddies. This fashion was not suited to the petite but venerated by the brawny who could knock down whole dinner queues in a single stampede.

My season came with the customised army bag, with a pencil case filled with markers and Tipp-Ex; this was a veritable khaki canvas to be intricately illustrated. Flowers and spirals, lyrics and tags, armoured with badges, adorned with patches: mine was a labour of love and a true work of wonder. I even made a bit of extra tuck money on the side, embellishing the bags of my fellow pupils.
Kate MacKay

Design

I reserve a fondness for all things kitsch and retro, but find it hard to wear such fabrics on a day-to-day basis. Some days I want sophistication, to not always stand out in the crowd.

I decided to mix the retro fabrics that I had found – either rummaging through my family's old sheets left over from when we were young or coming across something nostalgic in a charity shop – with something a little tamer to enable me to create an outfit that would not only be ultra hip but also ultra stylish.

Superhero bedspreads are a fantastic find, especially as with age they have a washed-out look that makes it easier to team them with a contrasting fabric. For this example I used *Star Wars* fabrics, found in a charity shop. I used heavy woollen tweed on top that I bought from my local fabric shop. Buying tweeds by the metre can sometimes turn into quite an expense so keep your eyes open for tweed trousers or jackets on your charity shop jaunts; this can work well in your final design as you have pockets and finished edges to add.

Fi MacKay

Materials

Second-hand stores, jumble sales and hand-me-downs

Outer: tough fabric such as tweed, denim or corduroy
Lining: quirky retro bedspreads
Stiffening: interfacing, canvas or tarpaulin
Bag strap or belt
Piping cord, wire or laces

Craft supplies

Pencil or chalk
Needle and thread / sewing machine
Scissors and pins
Fabric glue (optional)

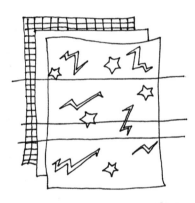

TIP:
How to make a bedspread record bag

The strap was taken from an old record bag, which you can buy from haberdashery shops but I prefer to use recycled materials as much as possible. The inner pocket was also taken from the same record bag, which saves precious time that would be wasted fussing over zip insertions and made the bag slightly more secure.

For this design the fabrics required stiffening as both were fairly flimsy. I used the heaviest weight of interfacing I could find, simply ironing it into position in order to strengthen the fabrics before commencing construction. Alternatively, you could use tarpaulin or canvas from another bag and sew this in between the chosen lining and outer fabric to create a sturdy bag. It's important to think about weather conditions, so the outer fabric from a record bag or old P.E. bag may be best as protection from wet conditions. Other outer fabrics that could be used are corduroy, jeans or leather. All of these fabrics can be easily sourced from charity shops, jumble sales, vintage stores and car boot sales. They are all relatively hard wearing and, if reconstructing trousers or a jacket for example, all embody pockets, zips and buttons that can be worked into your final design. Try to find jackets that are lined as you can incorporate this fabric into the design also (or save it for another creation).

When cutting the retro fabric, really take the time to think about what will be seen, I decided the flames of the pod racers should be visible as most of the fabric was actually plain blue. I find it was really effective in terms of the overall design to only give a hint as to where the fabric was originally derived from. Keep hold of the scraps as they could aid you in further creations. Maybe even try jazzing up an old dress or top by adding a funky collar or appliquéd design.

1   For this project I simply used a rectangle of fabric, dividing it into four parts and ending up with a sort of T-shape; as you might imagine a dice would be constructed.

> The front of the bag
> The base of the bag
> The back of the bag
> The lid of the bag

2   I decided I wanted this bag to be around the size of an A4 folder so I used that as a guide. I made the front lip of the bag slightly lower, the base only several inches deep, the back an inch higher and wider at both sides of the A4 folder and the top a mirror image of the base in size. This piece of fabric can then be reinforced at each fold, perhaps with piping cord or a couple of rows of stitching to really hold the shape. Two side pieces are also required; make sure they match the width of the base and the height of the front.

3   Cut all three fabrics to the exact same size and pin together. This bag is made in one piece that just folds together like a box. Mark across in soft pencil or in chalk where each section is, for example where the back of the bag will fall and where the lid of the bag will fall.

4   Decide which sides of the fabric are going to be seen both inside and outside and place them face to face, with the wrong sides facing, or the sides that will ultimately end up out of sight. Stitch with machine or by hand around the edge of these fabrics, leaving the top edge of the lid of the bag free from stitching. This allows the bag to be turned inside out, hiding all raw edges on the inside and protecting against fraying.

5   Where the marks have been mapped out, separating each section, sew along. This gives the bag structure. It is best to attach piping cord along these parts; laces could be used for example, or wire. If reinforcing in this way, be sure to set your machine to a zig-zag stitch so that a channel is formed with which to hold the wire in place, if sewing by hand, simply ensure you travel up the wire in a similar way, taking your first stitch up and then over the piping.

6   Pockets can be attached both outside and inside, and should be added before you attach the top and bottom layers of fabric unless you wish the stitching to show through in your final design. Save the buttons for future projects or attach them to the outside of the bag for further decoration.

7   I attached the strap of the bag at the end of its construction simply by sewing with the machine. However, a really strong needle is required as the fabric was so heavy. For ease, fabric glue could be used to hold in place.

Fi MacKay

Holding Court

❝The new urban street player
employs colour decoratively
and tactically, bringing a new
freshness to tennis attire❞

Holding Court

INCREASED ATHLETICISM, commercial demands and even global warming are factors that keep on-court fashion in perpetual flux. The modern tennis player is expected to exert powerful strokes, gymnastic leaps, underspins and slices without perspiring and retaining the level of chic required whilst ordinarily sipping a Pimms. The stark white linen institute, though still enforced at Wimbledon, has given way elsewhere to a new wave in style on the contemporary court. Sporting designers breathed a sigh of relief with the introduction of high heels rather than plimsoles, initiated by ex-ballroom-dancing tennis champ Deirdre Carr.

Colour is a big statement in the modern game, and though frowned upon by tennis authorities, the application of Tipp-Ex to grass stains mid-set is giving way to full costume changes. The new urban street player employs colour decoratively and tactically, using it to dazzle and confuse their opponent. Outfits are constructed in layers giving versatility of style, allowing quick changes and bringing a new level of freshness to tennis attire. It is now not uncommon to see up to twelve variations of the ensemble before 'love' has even been called. Independent sponsorship is of course a big factor in such a break from the classic regime. Dubbed 'walking bill-boards' by cynics, designers have artfully incorporated corporate colouring and slogans. In this outfit, Di has used iconic shopping bags to weave the bra, visor and waist band. The plastic gives great strength and flexibility of movement while repelling perspiration and advertising the local store.

Kate MacKay

Design

I love primary colours and bold geometric patterns. Mondrian, Picasso, cubism and art deco designs and patterns have always inspired me. So when the bold and colourful Lidl's supermarket bags caught my eye I couldn't resist playing with them, cutting them into strands and seeing what happened when I played at crocheting them into various shapes.

This fun holiday outfit is made up of plastic bags and a colourful scarf from my stash of charity shop finds. The bold primary colours of these elements were just made for each other. I made the hat first and liked it so much I decided to create an outfit for a scrap fashion show that Kate and I were planning. At the time, I was just heading off to the Findhorn Community (a unique spiritual and environmental centre in the north of Scotland) for an 'Experience Week'. Findhorn is a truly exceptional and inspirational place. Most of the outfit was made on the daily bus between the Cluny Hotel and the Findhorn Foundation. I was inspired and definitely in the flow of creativity!
Di Jennings

Materials

Second-hand stores, jumble sales and hand-me-downs

1 scarf

Your recycling

8 plastic bags

Craft supplies

Crochet hook
Needle and thread

TIP:

How to make the skirt from a scarf

1　Use a square scarf that you love! First I marked a circle in the middle of the scarf making the measurement of the circumference the same as the waist (or hips, if you intend it to be a hipster skirt like ours).

2　Then I cut out the circle and sewed the circumference of the remaining scarf to a waist band (or hip band).

3　Mine is made from strips of plastic crocheted from supermarket bags. You could also use a scrap of fabric or piece of wide elastic.

4　A stretchy fabric works best as there is no need for a zip. Be creative! Hey presto – a scarf skirt! So simple!

A stretchy fabric works best for the waistband as there is no need for a zip

TIP:

How to make a crocheted bra from plastic bags

1 Prepare the plastic bags for crocheting as described in the project 'Summer Collection' (see page 50). For the bra part of the bikini make 2 triangle-shaped pieces. I started by making a row of about 20 chain stitches to form the bottom of the triangle. Then I worked sequential rows of treble stitches and decreasing one stitch each row in the middle of the row as I worked. Keep an eye on how the bikini top is shaping up and if needed decrease some rows by two stitches. Make the second triangle the same as the first one and sew them together at the centre front.

2 To create the straps, work 4 long rows of chain stitches: one for each side of the bikini to tie at the back and attach the remaining 2 to the top of the triangle to tie around the neck. You now have a plastic bikini! My model complained bitterly about the feel of the plastic against this sensitive part of her anatomy, so I used the centre that I cut out of the scarf to make the skirt to line the bikini by cutting two triangles and hand stitched them into place. A satin-lined bikini – positively luxurious!

Di Jennings

Materials

Your recycling

6 plastic bags
Scraps from a scarf

Craft supplies

Crochet hook
Needle and thread

Patchwork Purses

' A great beginner's project, and an ideal way to use up scraps of left-over fabrics '

Patchwork Purses

THE FOOL IS AN INTRIGUING CHARACTER, outcast, poor but not to be pitied. He mocks society from its fringes, wearing his poverty in gaudy patches of rich fabrics. His is a suit of sewn-together fragments, a discordant array of old clothes; the once-treasured, now discarded status symbols of society.

The Fool appears at times of transition: Solstice, New Year, Easter and Beltane. Happy in the transience of things, from the outside looking-in he mocks our futile longing to cling to the feeble constructs we have created. Like his infinitely colourful costume, his speech, songs and dances are a jumble of parts collected, overheard and observed from the wealth of cultures he has passed by and through. Like a magpie he takes what he feels like and leaves what he doesn't. Be it a part of a story or a piece of cloth, he plays with each element he collects light-heartedly and arranges it with intent, always pleasing himself, making of it something new that is his all alone.

Therein lies his wisdom, he is a mediator between extremes. The fact that he is never in vogue means he is never out either. Never one to absorb or accept; what the world throws at him he instantly rejects. The Fool is a mirror of truth reflecting the madness of the blindly submissive; reminding all that even sanity is subjective, as futile as fashion and prey to the same fickle forces. His separateness affords him consistency and his madness permits him to not fear insanity. The fragments of truth that he stitches together seem to take his audience in nonsensical spirals but in the final instance, when he wraps up the tale all the clashing pieces come together in perfect harmony to make a new sense that common sense can't fathom. For as Shakespeare observed: 'The fool doth think he's wise, but the wise man knows himself to be a fool.'

Kate MacKay

Design

The bags and accessories started from a practical angle, deciding how best to use up and recycle a huge collection of fabrics and trimmings amassed over years of scouring jumble sales and charity shops. I especially love the fabrics used in vintage upholstery and home furnishings and have collected everything from tea towels and curtains to crimpolene blouses and ties. All are usually chosen for their bold prints and colours.

I generally sketch rough ideas for bag shapes and sometimes use old handbags for inspiration and as templates for patterns. I try to incorporate as many contrasting patterns and textures as possible while keeping the colourways the same. If your piece of fabric is very small you can cut out particular shapes from a print, like flowers or figures and then stitch on top of another print, perhaps incorporating buttons or braid to build a tactile 3D effect. I also like layering sheer or net fabrics over a different material and then cutting out shapes to reveal what's underneath.

Ideas generally evolve from the fabrics themselves and I like the finished product to be fun, individual and functional.

Kay Farnie

Materials

Second-hand stores, jumble sales and hand-me-downs

Scraps of bright nylon,
plastic, upholstery and vinyl
Zip or buttons
Ribbons and cord

Your Recycling

Scrap paper

Craft supplies

Scissors
Iron
Needle and thread

TIP:
How to design and make
a purse from recycled materials

This is a great beginner's project as it is small in scale, will be finished quickly and you will get a real sense of achievement. Get started by collecting the materials that you want to use.

Vinyls and plastics would be great at first – especially if you want to appliqué as no edge neatening is needed. Keep an eye out for discarded raincoats in different colours or an old shower curtain could work. I have also experimented with fusing together layers of supermarket plastic shopping bags. Build up several layers and use the iron to fuse them together – but make sure you have some paper between the iron and the top layer. You can create patterns by cutting small shapes and fusing them to the surface. You have to get the timing and heat just right – this requires some trial and error. But it creates a gorgeous half-melted organic-looking effect. I discovered this technique when I was making a mermaid costume for a community carnival. Her fins looked like spotty tropical fish made from brightly coloured melted plastic bags! If you have some clear plastic in your stash of goodies, create a window effect for a high tech look – how about putting a plastic toy inside for a fun effect? There is so much plastic that ends up in the bin heading straight to the tip – let's use some of it!

1   If you are working with fabric, collect the discarded garments you like for the colour and pattern. You are working on a small area so patterns need to be small – the impact of a larger scale design will get lost. Striking black and white geometrics are always a success, they are so smart. Stripes are fresh and it's such fun to create patterns with them when patch working. I have a purse made from fake fur off-cuts that I love – it has such a soft fluffy feel. Animal prints would work really well as they have such distinct small patterns and would look very stylish. I love the vintage furnishing fabrics that Kay has used for her purses.

2   Once you have gathered your materials decide on the shape of the purse. Do you want a rectangle, a square or maybe a circular purse? Look around in the shops at purse shapes that catch your eye and copy them. The purse can fasten with a zip, but there are other possibilities if sewing a zip feels a little daunting. If you make one side of the purse wider that the other it can fold over at the top and be fastened with a dome or a button and a loop. I love using Chinese frogs for fastenings…and it is very easy!

3   If this is your first project, a rectangle shape would be a simple start. Cut two identical rectangles to create your design.

4   I suggest that you put the zip in next. The side seams and bottom of the purse can be stitched last – make sure you leave a gap to enable you to turn the purse back out to the right side. Hand sew the gap to close it up – or machine stitch close to the edge of the purse if it is not too thick.

5   Once your sewing gets a bit more sophisticated I suggest lining the purse for a tidy finish inside.

TIP:
How to make a drawstring purse

This alternative drawstring design is even simpler to make.

1   Make the base of the purse a circle and cut a rectangle for the sides.

2   Stitch the long edge of the rectangle to create a tube shape.

3   Then stitch one end of the tube to the circle to create a round container shape.

4   This looks great with a drawstring to close it. You will need to create a 'casing' to thread the drawstring through. To do this, fold a wide hem over at the top and stitch in place. Then sew another line of stitching parallel to the former row and about ⅓ inch (1cm) apart. This is where you will thread the drawstring through. Start threading at the side seam for easy access.

A purse would make a great gift. You could design it to suit the taste and personality of your special friend. How lovely it would be receive an individually designed, recycled purse for Christmas…
Di Jennings

Duvet Dresses

Duvet Dresses

IN 1969 JOHN AND YOKO decided to transform the inevitable media circus that would accompany their honeymoon into a protest for World Peace. Interviewers were invited to the Amsterdam Hilton Hotel where the Liverpudlian singer-songwriter and Japanese contemporary artist famously said they would be 'talking in our beds for a week'. Thus the world witnessed its first 'bed-in'.

Such was the influence of these artists at the time that many feared a sudden economic decline caused by a predicted bout of copycat bed-ins. The expected slump in the workforce was such that a massive advertising campaign was planned to promote 'duvet attire' – the 'bed-in' for the peace protester about town. The idea was to encourage the public to incorporate their protest into the working day by wearing rather than taking to their beds. 'Bed-in Fridays' were a feature of the campaign, in which workers could swap their uniforms for a duvet outfit if they brought in £1 for the staff kitty on a Friday. Top models and designers were employed and an exclusive range of duvet work-wear and pillow millinery was set to hit the stores at the expected peak of the 'bed-in' backlash.

To the surprise of the heads of industries who might have experienced this 'duvet attire' first hand – and who seem to have been a bit out of touch culturally, the bed-in was met with cynicism and derision. Dismissed by the media as a publicity stunt it was largely ignored and certainly not replicated by the public. The 'duvet attire' range was pulled and the advertising campaign went unpublished.

The outfits pictured display some of the characteristic features of the range. Bold patterning and bright colours create impact while simple lines and clean cuts bring practicality and accessibility to the garment.

Kate MacKay

Design

We all have those days when we wish we could just stay in bed. Inspired by this cosy idea and the wonderful retro fabrics my Granny fashioned her guest room with, I decided to create summer dresses out of discarded bedspreads that would coax any *fashionista* out of slumber.

The lightweight nature of the material is brilliant for summery dresses, and the remnants can be used to create a simple bag to match or perhaps even flowers for your hair. Instant vintage that all will envy.

Fi MacKay

Materials

Hand-me-downs

Granny's retro duvet covers
Vintage dress pattern

Craft supplies

Scissors
Domestic sewing machine
Cotton thread
Lightweight interfacing

TIP:

How to work with a graded pattern

The 'coffee date' dress by Elaine May has a simple silhouette with a ruffle detail and just enough swing in the A-line skirt to make it dainty and feminine. It's quick and simple to make and very versatile – try it in a neutral colour with a cardigan for work, in navy silk for dinner out, in a fun print with a big belt for weekends or in black or fuchsia satin for a festive cocktail party.

The pattern – which can be found on the Alchemy Arts website at www.alchemyarts.org – is for standard sizes 2-10 US or 6-14 UK, with this sort of graded pattern I suggest making a mock-up of the basic bodice to test the fit. Also note that the pattern does not include seam allowances. I recommend adding a 1½ inch (around 4cm) seam allowance. Always refer to a size chart and always take careful measurements. The fashion industry knows all too well how far flattery can get you, resulting in real discrepancies in clothing sizing.

Always refer to a size chart and take careful measurements

TIP:

How to make a multi-size 'coffee date' dress

Instructions for a petite unlined, sleeveless dress with fitted bodice, scoop neck, A-line skirt, back zip and ruffle detail.

Pattern pieces:

1   bodice front (cut 1 on fold)
2   bodice back (cut 2)
3   bodice front facing (cut 1 on fold)
4   bodice back facing (cut 2)
5   skirt front (cut 1 on fold)
6   skirt back (cut 2)
7   ruffle (cut 1 strip of fabric 6 inches (15cm) wide x 36 inches (90cm) long, with fabric grain running lengthwise)

(*Note*: Cut out the ruffle line template. This is not a pattern piece, so do not cut a fabric piece for it; you will use this to transfer the ruffle line to the front of the bodice.)

Preparation:

1   Place pattern pieces on fabric, making sure the grain line is correct. Mark seam allowances. Cut pieces and transfer all markings to fabric.

2   Match centre of ruffle line template to centre of front bodice on right side of fabric. Points E and F should lie in the seam allowance, ⅛ inch (3mm) from the neck edge.

3   Mark ruffle line and all points on bodice front using tailor's chalk or transfer paper.

4   Apply lightweight interfacing to wrong side of facings. Stay stitch the neck and armhole edges.

Bodice:

1   Stitch front bodice darts and press darts towards centre. Trim dart excess if desired.

2   Stitch back bodice darts, press darts towards centre.

3   Stitch back bodice to front bodice at sides, right sides together. Press seam allowances open.

Ruffle:

1   Encase each long, raw edge of ruffle with a narrow zig-zag stitch. Fold in half lengthwise with right side on inside. Stitch short edges. Trim seam allowances on short edges. Turn right side out. Press.

2   Make a row of long stitches along the zig-zagged edge of ruffle through both layers of fabric, ¼ inch (7mm) from the edge. Make a second row parallel to the first, ½ inch (1½cm) from the edge. Pull threads to gather until the ruffle measures

21 inches (53 cm) in length. Tie threads to secure ends. Adjust gathers evenly.

Note: for the following part, it is easiest to pin and stitch each section of the ruffle to the bodice one at a time. However, it is a good idea to 'test pin' the entire ruffle in place, mark the ruffle where it meets each of the points, and unpin it before the following steps:

3 Pin one end of ruffle's gathered edge to point A on bodice front. Lay ruffle edge along ruffle line until point B.

4 Pin ruffle at point B. Baste or pin ruffle between points A and B. Stitch ruffle in place ¼ inch (7mm) from ruffle edge.

5 Fold ruffle back at point B and affix ruffle from point B to C in same fashion. Repeat until point E. (NB: be careful not to pull the ruffle too taut when attaching it, otherwise the bodice will pucker.)

6 Pin remaining ruffle from point E to point F, matching ruffle edge to the neck edge. Baste.

7 Stitch ruffle ½ inch (13mm) from neck edge (the stitching line lies in the seam allowance). Remove gathering threads from the ruffle.

Facing:

1 Sew bodice front facing and bodice back facing right sides together at the side seams.

2 Press seam allowances open. Trim seam allowances along lower edge and finish with a narrow zig-zag stitch, or finish lower edges of facing as desired.

3 Join the facing and bodice. This process will also close the shoulder seams and enclose the raw edge of the ruffle along the neckline.

Skirt:

1 Stitch skirt front to skirt back, right sides together. Press side seams open.

2 Stitch skirt to bodice, right sides facing, matching centres and side seams. Press seam allowances upwards towards the bodice.

Finishing:

1 Without catching bodice back facing, sew zipper to dress.

2 Stitch back skirt seam from bottom skirt edge to bottom of zipper. Press seam allowances open.

3 Fold in seam allowances on bodice back facing and press. Lay folded edges of facing over zipper tape and hand stitch to zipper tapes.

4 Tack facings to seam allowances. Tack ruffle in place if desired.

5 Sew hook and eye in place at back neck opening.

6 Try on dress. Mark hem at desired length. Hem as desired.

Design by Elaine M. Huang

Try it in a neutral with a cardigan for work, or in a fun print with a big belt for weekends

Lady
Lavender

‘This dress has a flapper feel;
it makes a great party dress
when I feel like playing at
being a "lady"! ,

Lady Lavender

TO BE NEAR THE FRAGRANT FIELDS of Provence is to know why lavender has always been associated with romance. Now associated with old ladies, lavender could be described as the Viagra of yesteryear, such was the belief in its aphrodisiac qualities. The ancient Greek Anacreon recommended that the breasts be anointed with lavender since it was said they were the seat of the heart. On St Luke's day, young Tudor girls would sip lavender dew and whisper, 'St Luke, St Luke be kind to me, in my dreams let my true love see,' and suitors would pledge lavenders blue to their dears or 'dillies'.

As one not famed for an amorous nature, surprisingly Queen Victoria was a great lavender enthusiast. So much so that she appointed Miss Sarah Sprules 'Purvey of Lavender Essence to the Queen'. This lady-in-waiting-come-sex-counsellor would spend the languid days selecting blossoms from the royal lavender lawns. The finest ones would be spun into silk sheets, woven with silver threads and crushed into fragrant oils with which to sweeten the royal breath and adorn the royal boudoir and bosom for the pleasure of Prince Albert. Nine children later, this common shrub certainly seemed to have worked for this dour-looking couple (although it is entirely possible that there was an associative aphrodisiac effect at work, akin to the notion that oysters, due to their shape, have virility-offering properties). Pale-skinned and slender, dressed in light silks and pearls, perhaps young Sarah Sprules was privy to more essence than lavender alone.
Kate MacKay

Design

When I moved to Scotland to live, I found that I was attracted to a gentler palette than I had used in New Zealand, which reflected the softer quality of the Scottish light. This dress is inspired by the soft lavenders and pinks of the gorgeous flowers that blossom in springtime.

 The dress has a flapper feel that harks back to my favourite era: the 1920s. It is a relatively simple design and makes a great party dress when I feel like playing at being a 'lady'! I could not resist the beaded top when I saw it at a market – it was just too gorgeous to pass by. When I got home I discovered that it worked beautifully with a couple of scarves in my stash of collected goodies at home. The skirt is made of the two scarves and the dress is finished with draped fabric off-cuts at the hip and is decorated with jewellery bits 'n' bobs. The headdress is made from a scarf and is also decorated with a necklace. The outfit is completed with a choker.

Di Jennings

Materials: headdress

Second-hand stores, jumble sales and hand-me-downs

Long scarf
Coloured glass necklace or beads

Craft supplies

Needle and thread

Materials: choker

Second-hand stores, jumble sales and hand-me-downs

1 fabric scrap
1 ribbon
Beads, pearls or decorative beads

TIP:
How to make a headdress from a scarf

1   There are so many ways to play with a scarf to make it into a headdress. On this occasion, the scarf was a long one with tassels at each end so I decided to use them as a feature at the back of the headdress.

2   The scarf was about the right length to wrap twice around the head with a few twists. I twisted the scarf loosely and stitched it at intervals to hold the twists loosely on place.

3   Finally I threaded a coloured glass necklace around the headdress and stitched it to the headdress at intervals.

TIP:

How to make a choker from scraps

1 I often make a choker from left-over scraps to finish off my outfits. For the Lady Lavender I started by making a narrow band about ¾ inch (2cm) wide from a fabric off-cut in the same fabric that was used on the dress.

2 To create the 2 cm wide band, I cut the width 1½ inches (4cm) plus seam allowances and made the length the neck measurement plus about 2 inches (5cm) for overlap and seam allowances. I folded this in half lengthwise and stitched around the raw edges, leaving a gap in the middle of the long edge to turn the band through to the right side. I used a knitting needle to push the corners out and then hand stitched the gap. Finally I ironed the band to flatten the seams.

3 The narrow piece of ribbon was twice as long as the band so I gathered it to create a frilly effect before hand stitching it lengthwise to the neckband.

4 It still looked a little unfinished and I always think a choker needs a bauble or two. Fortunately I had some mauve glass beads left over so I hand stitched them along the centre of the ribbon.

5 Finally I used a hook and eye to fasten the choker at the back of the neck. It looks so pretty and feminine! I like to design and make accessories after the main parts of the garment are well developed. That way I know what materials are leftover and design chokers, armbands, leggings etc to suit. 'Cut your coat according to your cloth,' I hear my mother say...

Di Jennings

> I often make a choker
> from left-over scraps to
> finish off my outfits

Pretty Pinny

❛Get the apron out of the
kitchen and out into the world
where it belongs❜

Pretty Pinny

WORK WEAR IS THE PERFECT PLAYING FIELD for rebellious creativity. When the uniformed mass is fractured by individual tweaks and embellishment, magic is brought into the mundane and art is brought into life – what better place to start than with the humble pinny? Household washing machines have today rendered the working housecoat redundant, giving way to the new line in statement aprons. Any desperate housewife would be only too pleased to answer the door to her guests dressed in this apron apparel but apron etiquette must be adhered to. The pinny should be removed as your guests enter the door, demonstrating that you favour the 'hands on' approach to housekeeping but are also bohemian enough to not have noticed the time. The pinny should remain on when answering the door to postman, milkman, hawkers or traders to whom you want to convey that you run a tight ship, if you are having an affair with the person at the door keep the pinny on in front of the neighbours and allow your 'Mr-ess' to remove it for you when indoors.

The form of the classic waist apron is coy, offering limited protection, so it is best suited to light dusting and other less strenuous housework. This is the kind of apron worn by the chatty, socialite housewife who has her own maid and can be accessorised with marigold gloves in yellow or pink. Long ribbons not only secure the waist apron, they can enhance the figure and offer a range of silhouettes depending on the tightness of tying and where you place the bow. If you are attempting housework a plain back bow or French knot (to the side) is more practical, for answering the door a front bow can be refreshing. The elegant woman with a lot on her mind expresses that she is such with an array of polishing paraphernalia carefully incorporated into her apron design. Dusters need not be unsightly if arranged beside complementary handkerchiefs and doilies. J-cloths have delightful blue candy stripes that – when picked up by a cobalt necklace or silk Prussian blouse – can be positively delicious-looking and a copper wire brush glinting in the sunlight is practically an ornament in itself.

Kate MacKay

Design

Pardonnez-moi... It is my personal mission to get the apron out of the kitchen and out into the world where it belongs. Wear it as a layer over jeans, leggings or a skirt...add a fun bit of colour and a pattern to make a 'ho-hum' outfit stand out. This colourful cotton/linen/polyester apron is designed from three skirts, the bottom piece of a vintage 1930s rayon dress and a colourful 1950s crocheted doily.

Two floral prints sit atop of a ruffled black, pink and white pleated ruffled bottom. The doily became a pocket. The reverse is a 1930s novelty rayon print with architectural images and dancers. The tie is grosgrain ribbon topped with vintage pink metallic ric-rac. It measures 24 inches (60cm) wide, 17 inches (43cm) high and the ties measure 96 inches (2m 45cm) from end to end. I make long ties so that my aprons fit a variety of sizes. Hand wash and hang to dry.

I tend to work in surges. I recently had an apron surge and pulled out a whole drawer full of potential apron parts and pieces that I'd been collecting and organizing over the past year. Skirts, salvaged vintage fabrics, Mexican embroidered appliqués, crochet trim, ties and belts. The resulting collection is about as eclectic as you might imagine...not dissimilar to the contents of one's recipe box. So I decided to name each one for the edible concoction that it brought to mind and tagged each with a mini-recipe card with its 'ingredients'. Fourteen aprons, each one-of-a-kind with its unique personality. Inspired by my flickr and real life friend, graygoosie, I am determined to earn the apron its rightful position in the public domain. Graygoosie hosts an 'Apron Outfits' group on flickr where members post pictures of themselves in their aprons. So if you wonder where or how you'd wear an apron, check out her group for inspiration. They're like a scarf in terms of their flexibility and a great way to brighten up an outfit.

What's your image? Is it something you've thought about? How do your clothes reflect who you are? I enjoy the idea of creating a new persona through fashion. Some days colourful, other times subtle: feminine on Saturday, edgy on Wednesday. So that's how I design...for the woman who isn't in a fashion box nor wants to be defined in a particular way.

Lori Marsha

Materials

Second-hand stores, jumble sales and hand-me-downs

Pretty pieces of retro fabric
Scraps of tassels, trimming
Linen and lace to embellish

Craft supplies

Scissors
Needle and thread

TIP:
How to make a decorative pinny

Getting started

Think romantic, pretty florals and old lace *à la* Laura Ashley. I suggest that you collect recycled skirts, dresses etc in these pretty fabrics. Don't worry about the shape of the garments – you will deconstruct them. It's the patterns and colours of the fabric that matter. Add some lace doilies and placemats. They will be useful for trims and pockets.

Or alternatively you could go 'fruity' – I like the idea of a colourful apron covered in apples and oranges…or maybe strawberries! Another possibility is using white elements and adding frills to the pinny for a sexy French maid look! I have also made fun aprons from vinyl off-cuts – this is great as the seams need no finishing and it lends itself to simple appliqué. I remember making one with a big smiley face for the barbeque cook. Whatever theme you decide on, make a pile of elements that work together – another 'sea of stuff'!

1   Start by deconstructing your larger garments. If you have a gathered skirt, cut away the waistband. If you are deconstructing a dress, cut away the sleeves. Turn the garments into flat pieces of fabric. Keep all the off-cuts as they will be useful for trims/pockets – or for future projects.

2   Unless you are a skilled pattern maker I suggest that you use an existing pinny that you like the shape of as a starting point. You may have a piece of fabric from your deconstruction that is big enough for the main part of the pinny. If not cut and join several segments – place any seams to look like side seams if possible! If you have several smaller pieces I suggest that you make a patchwork – vertical panels could look good. The pieces need to be wider at the bottom than the top if you want to create an A-line shape. When patchworking, fabrics with small patterns work better than large designs.

3   Make the measurement along the top of the apron equal to your waist measurement. Sew a couple of waist darts, or curve the top of side seams to shape the waist to hip area.

4   Cut the pinny as long as you want – a butcher's style apron needs to be long and straight, but a saucy French maid pinny is best kept short with curved edges and a frill added all the way around the outer edge. Have a play with shapes in front of the mirror. Cut, slash and pin initially – don't be afraid to experiment.

The pocket

1   I would always put a pocket on a pinny – there is nothing worse than having nowhere to put those bits 'n' bobs when tidying, vacuuming and dusting! The pocket can be a creative design feature. See what off-cuts and decorative elements you have that will work. If your pinny has square lines make a square or rectangular pocket. If your apron is curvy and frilly make a round-shaped pocket. Try a large centre pocket – or maybe a jaunty single side pocket or even a pocket on each side. It will depend upon the elements you have to work with. You can patchwork, appliqué, embroider as your heart desires.

2   To create a finished edge for the pocket, cut a lining piece the same shape as the pocket, place right sides together and sew around the outside, leaving a gap to pull through to the right side before pressing flat and sewing to the pinny around the sides and bottom. Try adding a small frill of fabric or lace around the edge of the pocket – if you do this it is best to round off the corners of the pocket first.

3   Finish the pinny with a waistband. Ensure that you make it long enough to extend beyond the pinny and create enough length to tie into a bow around the waist. If you do not have a long enough piece of fabric, join some shorter pieces. Now you are pretty as a picture in your pinny so get out those marigold gloves (matching of course!) and that feather duster and get down to it!

Di Jennings

Chapter 4:

Winter Woollens

Fuzzy Felts

JOSEPH BEUYS worked to push the world of the contemporary artist out of the gallery away from the elite, aiming to be all that one who transforms materials can be: an artist, activist, alchemist and shaman. A practitioner in the art of transformation, this 'science of freedom' afforded Beuys the vertiginous liberty to move between identities and teeter on the edges of actuality and fantasy. As a German experiencing post-war devastation and guilt, Beuys set out to systematically transform harsh realities into a myth of his own making. The protagonist in his story was himself: wandering lost whilst serving in the war as a gun pilot from 1941–1945, Beuys's plane crashed and, surrendering to hypothermia, he 'died'. His body was found by a nomadic tribe of Tartas who rolled him up in the vastly sprawling blanket of felt with which they make their homes. Cocooned in this warm woollen womb, Beuys was resurrected into a new reality which he began to explore with the tactile nature of a newborn child.

He created playful objects, attire and installations with felt, his magical, protective and life-giving material; a piano shrouded in soft silence, a hanging suit that echoes with emptiness and strong and high copper-topped pillars. One of his most famous and radical 'Actions' was entitled 'I Love America and America Loves Me,' which took place in May 1974. Beuys landed in New York and was immediately wrapped in felt and carried by ambulance to the gallery in which his Action would take place. In a bid to insulate and isolate himself, swathed in felt he didn't see or touch American soil until he reached the gallery room in which he would spend the next three days along with his felt blanket, gloves, a staff and a living coyote. In Native American culture the coyote had been revered as a powerful god, a creature that could move between the realms of the physical and spiritual spheres. European settlers viewed the coyote as a pest, a beast of vermin to be exterminated. Each day of the Action, Beuys was delivered fifty copies of the *Wall Street Journal* which the coyote would urinate on. At the end of the Action, Beuys was once again swathed in felt and returned to the airport.
Kate MacKay

Design

This range of brooches and hairclips is made on a domestic knitting machine. All are knitted with donated lamb's wool and cashmere sweaters, before being felted, or they are made from recycled wool which, after felting, is cut and hand sewn.

The mittens are knitted on a Design-A-Knit machine with my own patterns, part felted and sewn together. The basic sewing is very easy to do and the mittens can be made from any knitted fabric, be it your own or scrap sourced from other locations. I find second-hand cashmere or pure wool jumpers great for cutting up and crafting into new and unique accessories.

As with all my work, the primary inspiration comes from the environment, both natural and manmade. I became fascinated with photographing manmade elements of the world and developing designs from the fantastic mix of patterns and textures found within our natural and synthetic environments. Botanic gardens are my favourite source of inspiration as they perfectly combine the wildness of nature with the organization and control of man's invention. A huge inspiration is also land art and the fascinating work of taking art back to nature and creating manmade objects in the landscape using only natural materials. (Land art was the focus of my dissertation whilst at university and particularly the work and methods of Andy Goldsworthy and Richard Long.)

Felting is one of the most important processes involved in my projects, as I couldn't cut up and hand stitch knitted pieces without it. Felting involves fusing together the stitches of knitted fabrics through a washing process so that it shrinks and no longer frays. My materials and equipment list is quite basic as I don't have access to a studio and do all my work from home. My lovely domestic knitting machine is a prized possession, found in perfect condition in a charity shop for £30! A washing machine is handy, though I often use the sink to hand wash, as it saves electricity and energy – much more eco friendly. High quality wool is a must: cashmere, lamb's wool, merino and glenshear are the best. Then, you simply need scissors, thread and needles for sewing. A knitting machine is not an essential as material can be sourced, ready to felt and start crafting.

Jo McCall

Materials

Second-hand stores, jumble sales and hand-me-downs

Pure wool knitwear in any shape or form (only pure wool will felt)

Craft supplies

A basin and lots of hot, soapy water and lots of time and patience
A washing machine for those needing instant gratification
Fabric scissors
Needle and thread
Tailor's chalk

TIP:
How to source knit materials

Making or customizing your own knitwear is so easy! Firstly it depends on the source of your material. Sourcing high quality materials from ethical and inexpensive sources is also important to me. Few people own a knitting machine, so as an alternative, charity shops are great sources of second-hand knitwear; living in Edinburgh thankfully provides me with fantastic charity shops, as well as a great second-hand fabric shop called Borders Scrap Store in Musselburgh – and there are always unwanted hand-me-downs from friends.

Part of the reason I use lamb's wool, cashmere and merino is that they are some of the only wools that will felt well and once washed, create a beautiful 'handle' – a felter's term for the touch and texture of the fabric. Once felted, a knitted fabric can decrease in size by over a third and this differs for every wool and wash, so always experiment first, and allow more material than you think you need.

TIP:
How to make felt

1   Step one, once you have your sourced or knitted material, is felting. Felt can be hand made from raw fibres by layering the fibres horizontally and vertically alternately, covering with a lace tablecloth and applying lots of hot soapy water and hand scrubbing until the fibres fuse together to produce a fabric. This is labour intensive and time consuming but very effective. Alternatively, a piece of fabric can be felted by washing. Unfortunately there is no exact instruction to the specifications of washing as every fabric and wool requires a different temperature and intensity of wash to felt. To part-felt, simply fill a sink or basin with very hot water and a little washing powder, add the material and scrub it together until it begins to felt. It is not just the temperature of the water that felts but the friction on the fabric so consistently rubbing it together is necessary. You will get nowhere by placing the fabric in boiling water and stirring it, but equally it won't have any effect by rubbing in cold water.

2   Part-felting can be used to produce a 'slightly felted' effect and gives the material a soft texture but it will still fray when cut. I have always used a washing machine to felt, so that all the stitches fuse together and it can be cut up. This is where experimentation is required; some wool will felt on a 30 degree cycle, whereas others could require a 60 degree spin cycle. When testing new wools, I generally start with a standard 40 degree wash to see the effect. However, if you are using sourced fabric, for example, a jumper bought in a charity shop; it is likely to need a hotter, faster wash, as many manufactured clothes are treated with chemicals to prevent shrinkage. As mentioned above, friction is also important, fabrics often felt better when combined in the wash with a towel.

TIP:
How to make felt jewellery

After the felting, the rest of the design process is simple. Your fabric can now be cut up in whatever way you please.

1   To make the jewellery, I simply cut the fabric into strips, then, for the spiral accessories, combine two colours and roll them together before hand sewing (carefully so the thread doesn't show) or layer the strips around each other and sew to create a corsage effect.

2   To finish them, I have hair and brooch clips which are sewn on by hand. Most companies require a large minimum order but the website I use is www.thebeadshop.com, which allows you to purchase all manner of jewellery-making equipment in small quantities.

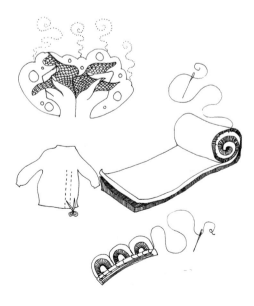

Fleecy Mitts

Fleece is such an easy material
to work with as it doesn't fray
at all: just cut it into whatever
shape you like 9

Fleecy Mitts

THE GLOVE is a many-faceted five-pronged distal phalanges sheath that is utilitarian, decorative or symbolic. A black synthetic lace glove might leave the fingers suggestively nude, offering modest protection to the palm, whilst a leather-cushioned boxing glove swallows the hand up completely making the wearer feel as if their fist has been upholstered. The rubber glove or 'marigold', as it is affectionately termed, is the Wellington boot of the wrist. Favoured by housewives as a precaution against prune palm, the marigold is like the Wellington in that it is used in wet conditions, never really fits and leaves a lingering rubbery scent about the person. Unlike the Wellington, the marigold is predominantly destined to remain indoors, like the reading glove and bath mitten. It is difficult to perform acts of precision when wearing marigolds, just as it would be hard to perform ballet wearing Wellies. The artisan is advised to opt instead for the kid glove.

Made from the fine soft leather from baby Alpine goats, the kid glove steadies the hand, is supple, delicate and offers excellent grasp. The 'kid' is the glove favoured by trades of exactitude. To be able to 'handle with kid gloves' is to the bomb diffuser what being 'sure-footed as a mountain goat' is to the fell runner. The fell runner himself has as little need for gloves as he seems to have for trousers, shirts and the other trappings of civilised society. If he were to be encouraged to work 'hand in glove', it would only ever be by some sort of gortex knuckle-strapping glove that monitored his speed. This so-called sports glove would never be the appropriate glove with which to start a fight. To throw down the gauntlet requires something far more imposing, with large hands and coverage up to the elbow, you want to say to your enemy: 'Look at the size of my glove! There's going to be two of them round your neck pretty soon if you're not careful!'. A falconry glove would suffice, a silk opera glove would not, elbow length though it may be.

Kate MacKay

Design

It was getting cold in my studio/workshop/garage. Even if the fog burns off and the day warms up, unless it gets really hot, my workshop stays pretty cool. Which isn't so bad, but my hands get cold and I can't stand cold hands!

I had been coveting a pair of knitted hand warmers since last winter and had got all sorts of fabulous favourites online, but I hadn't found exactly what I was looking for in terms of colour and style. Then a friend went and knitted up a gorgeous pair of mittens (see http://houseonthehillroad.typepad.com) and that really sent me over the edge – I wanted to knit some too! The voice of reason warned me that the knitted mitten project should wait, as I am perpetually consumed by the never-ending knit scarf (which I still love!) and definitely don't have the skills yet for anything as challenging as the mittens.

But as I was thinking about my cold hands and coveting (as I do) my friend's pair, I remembered a pair of Old Navy fleece gloves that I had crammed into a drawer in my dresser. I hardly ever wore them and I thought I might be able to make them at least *partially* cute.

Carrie Sommers

Materials: hand warmers

Second-hand stores, jumble sales and hand-me-downs

Pair of fleece gloves
Scraps of felt
Faux pearl beads

Craft supplies

Embroidery floss or thread
Fabric scissors
Needle

Materials: felting

Second hand stores, jumble sales and hand-me-downs

Pure wool garment to felt

Craft supplies

Needle and thread
Tailor's chalk
Fabric scissors

...accessorise with a big mug of hot chai!

TIP:
How to turn fleece gloves into stylish hand warmers

Fleece is such an easy material to work with as it doesn't fray at all. As with felt you can cut it into whatever shape you like without fear of the material unravelling, so the stitching in this project is gratuitous decoration only, bliss! Start by cutting off the fingers and thumb, then whip stitch or blanket stitch around the cut open top and thumb holes using ordinary embroidery floss in a colour that complements your gloves...simple.

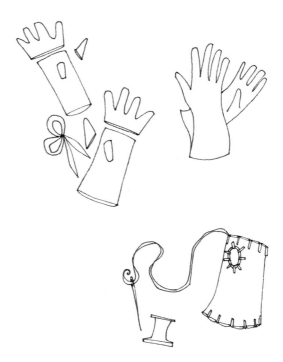

TIP:
How to embellish on fleece

1   Adapting the glove shape was easy but I still thought they were a bit boring. Initially, I started to embroider little flowers on the top, but my flowers didn't quite turn out the way I visualised, and despite fleece being easy to cut and stitch, I discovered that you can't really draw or trace on it, so I had to think of something else.

2   My solution was to cut out little flowers from felt and stitch them to the fronts of the mittens. Again, when you do this use a complementary colour; I used ivory to match the embroidery floss. You could make them more varied than mine; it's a great use for little off-cuts of felt.

3   Add little faux-pearl beads to the centres of your felted blossoms, and a little running stitch for the stem...I advise that you accessorise with a big mug of hot chai! *Mmmm* perfect!

Carrie Sommers

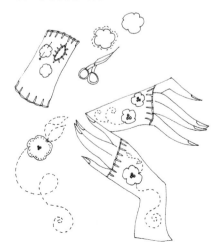

TIP:
How to make felt mittens

1   Making your own mittens is very simple. The knitted fabric needs only part-felting as you want to retain flexibility and elasticity. Once you have achieved the desired handle cut the length you would like leaving about a ½ inch (1½ cm) seam allowance, if needed, at either end.

2   Then fold over the ends and sew along the seams. If you don't have an over locker, a zig-zag stitch is most effective for holding the seam.

3   After this, you need measurements for your hand span, wrist and forearm. Mark these measurements on the length of fabric (the mittens can be any length you like from wrist to elbow or longer). Use tailor's chalk for the markings, then sew the seam on the reverse. I machine sew as it is stronger and less time consuming, but if you don't have a sewing machine then they can also be hand sewn.

4   Finally, for a thumb-hole, turn the mittens the right way out and try them on. Once on, stretch out your hand a little and mark on the gap between the thumb and forefinger, then sew around ½ inch (or 1½cm) down on this mark to make a thumb-hole. Hey presto, you have effectively made recycled mittens! They make great presents and also are an amazing winter accessory.

Jo McCall

Reworked
Coats

❝This 1950s herringbone tweed coat was restored with French velvet, feminine bows and oversized polka dot buttons❞

Reworked Coats

JAPAN IS A TAILORED ISLAND made from tightly woven wefts of people and cities cut and hung in perfect harmony. The 'Tailor of Japan' has an eye for detail and a heart of precision, unruly threads and jagged hems of nature are patiently coaxed into the bridges and falls of the impeccably cut cloth. From its conception a tree is guided by the Tailor of Japan, sinews spun and snipped to a design that portrays the very essence of the perfect tree, its core twisted and pulled to give the impression of a life growing against the perfect breeze. Matter and meaning are reshaped rather than discarded, 'It's not the fabric that you wear but how you wear it!' says the sign in the window of the Tailor's workshop.

The past is not something to be escaped or buried, the present is something to be carefully smoothed and lovingly cared for, mended and made into an archetype elevated to the status of eternity. The skill of the Tailor is such that a ragged cloth can become an Emperor's robe; a whore can become a Geisha and a murderer a Samurai. It seems that wayward misfortune and erratic chance would have no place in the Tailor's studio, but on the contrary they form the very basis of his work. Rolled out on the bench, the unsightly edges are trimmed, a pattern is marked out with precision and intent, placed to make the most of the best features and to disguise the weak. The feeling is that each work is created forever; nothing is impermanent or throw-away. Every gesture is a lifetime's work, taking the elements on offer and tightly working them together to make a stronger, more beautiful and perfect whole. Men visit the Tailor to have the body they were given adorned with the stories they have lived until the blank canvas of flesh is completely submerged beneath the bloody fresco. A lace curtain of tattoos artfully sprawls across their figure, whole manuscripts carved into the back along the arms and legs, each new story fitting into the last, growing out of it into a body of work.

Kate MacKay

Design

Our culture glorifies the new. Trendy garments with built-in obsolescence quickly lose appeal when they appear on the 'What's not...' side of the 'What's hot...' fashion column. So they are relegated to the back of the closet, stuffed into a bottom drawer and, if they are not dumped into the trash, they eventually find their way to thrift and consignment stores where they languish under the humiliation of multiple markdowns and overpopulated racks.

As every savvy recycler knows, treasure often hides between purple power suits and polyester broomstick skirts. And the thrill of finding a mustard Dupioni silk blouse or a fine gauge British wool dress makes the sometimes exhaustive searches worthwhile. I am proud to say that I design all of my garments from recycled materials. They begin their lives in other forms. A skirt morphs into a dress and a dress is divided among three new dresses, an undergarment moves outside. I compare this redefining of garments to the joy of an unexpected adoption, the designer dog abandoned by the socialite, then loved dearly by the little boy whose parents finds her at the pound. Under the right conditions, abandoned possessions live a fuller second life.

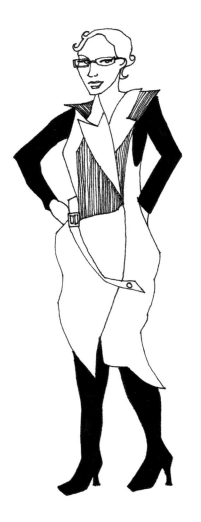

This Parisienne-inspired 1950s herringbone tweed coat was salvaged and restored with French velvet embroidered panels, feminine bows and oversized polka dot buttons. The velvet collar and cuffs add to the sophisticated charm.

Lori Marsha

TIP:
How to add a bit of flair

1 Give an old coat a new lease of life by adding new collars or cuffs. Velvet and fake fur have always been popular choices, but I have also used winter scarves, pieces of tapestry, quilting or embroidery.

2 Alternatively, just covering the existing collar and/or cuffs with a luxury fabric can be quick and look fabulous. If your coat is made of wool some embroidery on the edges can look great. A large blanket stitch in a contrasting colour is very effective.

3 Making a detachable collar and cuffs to compliment your coat is a great way to experiment with versatility without having to fully commit to the transformation. You can attach buttons, Velcro or laces to tie them on.

4 An unusual idea for giving a straight 'boxy' coat some 50s flair is to cut up the centre back and insert a godet (triangular shape) to create a flared back (see 'Spiralling Elegance', Chapter 7). It is important to get a good colour match. My coat was black and even though the shade was not identical it was not noticeable because of the different angles where the godet was inset into the coat.

5 Creating asymmetry can also be very stylish. If the coat is too big, just move buttons to the side and *voila*! An a-symmetrical coat. Try adding a half belt to the back of a coat. If the coat lacks shape adding a belt can gather the fabric and create a slimmer silhouette, or the belt section can be placed at angles to create an unusual figure.

Di Jennings

Materials

Second-hand stores, jumble sales and hand-me-downs

Old coat(s)
Buttons, braid, trinkets and trimmings
Scraps and off-cuts of velvet, fake fur, tartan and tweed

Craft supplies

Scissors
Needle and thread

Turtle Neck Bag

This project is perfect for recycling the shrunken cashmere sweater you accidentally boil washed

Turtle Neck Bag

IT'S HARD TO IMAGINE that St Clement, the patron saint of hatters, was once just a humble peasant boy with nothing more than an eye for textiles to make him stand out from the crowd. From a young age, Clement demonstrated particular flair in the field of fabrics. He was the first to notice the grain of the weave and would show the other peasants how best to tie their togas in order to fully emphasise the hang of the cloth. Sadly, artistic boys were as persecuted then as they are today and Clement's sense of style did not rest easy with the local yobs.

One day while being chased by his enemies Clement's feet became unbearably painful. He was wearing his sister's sandles as he felt they better complemented his soft muslin slip, a decision that he was cursing now as they were no good to run in. Thankfully for Clement (and for generations of hatters), he managed to give his enemies the slip. He bathed his blistered feet in a cool mountain stream and bound them in sheep's wool to ease the pain on the long walk home. To Clement's amazement, when he returned his sandles to his awaiting sister a miracle occurred. The friction of the sandles as he walked and the warmth of his tired wet feet had felted the sheep's wool into beautiful little boots. Even the yobs were astounded, a whole new realm of woollen wear was in store. Warm woollen vests replaced draughty cotton togas, snugly fitting scull caps replaced impractical laurel crowns and everyone rejoiced, their hearts full of joy and as warm as their cosy slipper-clad toes. To this day St Clement brings protection to hatters and felt artists everywhere and is celebrated with great feasting every year on 23rd November.

Kate MacKay

Design

I was given a beautiful Scandinavian jumper by a woman I met at the Edinburgh Guild of Weavers, Spinners and Dyers. She had qualms about the fact that the neck was an awkward cross between a turtle and a polo neck. I realised that, as my mother would say, it 'did nothing for me' and so resolved to reincarnate the jumper as a bag. I love wooden/unusual handles on any bag and am equally enthusiastic when the fabric used to make them has interesting knitted patterns, so I frequently adapt the shape of a bag to use these two factors to maximum effect. Felting reinforces the fabric as the fibres are drawn closer together, making it stronger – but not quite strong enough for transporting encyclopaedias.

As well as clunky wooden handles, I am inspired by kitsch jumpers, unusual bag shapes and Fair Isle patterns in particular. These bags make me want to skip and swing my bag jauntily. Or run away to Copenhagen (any excuse)…

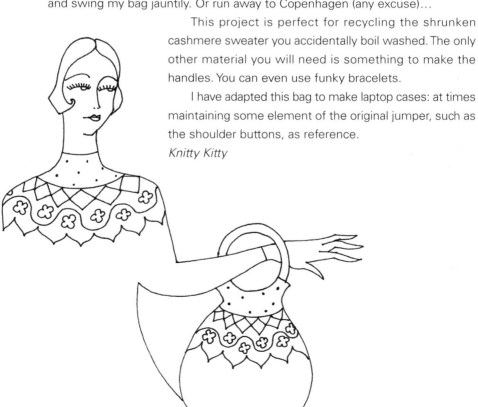

This project is perfect for recycling the shrunken cashmere sweater you accidentally boil washed. The only other material you will need is something to make the handles. You can even use funky bracelets.

I have adapted this bag to make laptop cases: at times maintaining some element of the original jumper, such as the shoulder buttons, as reference.

Knitty Kitty

Materials

Hand-me-downs, second-hand stores and jumble sales

1 pure wool jumper (NOT machine washable)
Bag handles or large bracelets
Alternatively make a leather strap by reusing an old belt or dog leash!

Craft supplies

Washing machine, laundry detergent and fabric softener
Basic sewing materials: needle, thread, scissors, dressmaker's chalk

TIP:
How to make a felted bag

1 Find a pure wool jumper of pleasing colours/patterns or begrudgingly accept the feasting of moths on an existing piece of knitwear (provided it hasn't been too badly savaged).

2 Machine boil wash (60 degrees plus) the jumper with a small amount of detergent and fabric softener.

3 It is often advisable to include another item in the wash. Hardy garments which can withstand these temperatures are good company for woollens as the friction aids the felting process.

4 If you have a top-loading machine, you have the advantage of checking on the progress of the wash from time to time. Otherwise, occupy yourself for the duration of the wash. It's a nerve-wrecking time awaiting the final outcome. There's always an element of risk that comes with felting: many an afternoon has been spent in anticipation of the results of this sacrificial shrinkage! Felting time varies depending on the temperature, the type of water in your area and also the type of detergent used. Also bear in mind that some fabrics call for multiple cycles for maximum felting. In the ideal finished felted article, individual knitted stitches cannot be distinguished: the fabric has a weightier, denser feel to it.

5 If possible stop the machine before a spin cycle: take the excess moisture out of the felted garment with a towel and lay it flat to dry. My mother remembers her mother, a professional knitter, leaving finished damp projects wrapped in newspaper under the hearth rug, where the family's footsteps would serve to flatten down the garment! In this case, leave the garment out to air-dry and adjust the shape if necessary.

6 Once dry, lay the jumper flat. Using dressmaker's chalk, sketch out the bag shape you require (remembering to leave a seam allowance: extra space on the outside of the stitching). Usually the jumper shape best lends itself to a square or rectangular shaped bag. (Disregard the arms for a later project: a matching purse? Or wrist-warmers?)

7 Depending on the degree of shrinkage and the shape/size of bag you require, the new width of the jumper's 'chest' can be just the right size for your bag. In this case, just a row of stitches along the bottom will complete the body of the bag. You can take advantage of ribbing often found along the bottom of jumpers to use as extra reinforcement for the bag's base: doubling it up on itself so you have 2 layers of ribbing at the bottom. Stitch securely in place. A strip of cardboard can be added to the base of the finished article to define the shape and add structure.

8 In the case of the Scandinavian jumper, I made a feature of the famous 'awkward' neck! This can naturally form a handle shape: you simply need to put 2 small cuts in the sides of the neck/ribbing so you can turn down it down to catch the handles. Holding or pinning the handles in place, stitch the neck down to secure.

9 If you wish to use an old belt/dog leash for longer straps, use 'O' or 'D'-shaped metal rings to secure it: doubling the leather back on itself through this, stitching together, or simply stitching the leather to the bag itself. Remember that the heavier the load you transport in the finished bag, the more of a toll it will take on the wool.

10 Alternatively, you can cut the bag shape strategically so that the neck ribbing become the handles themselves. You can include or transplant any additional features of the original jumper as a form of homage: pockets can be attached or indeed fashioned from excess fabric, shoulder buttons/ epaulettes included, or if the jumper has a particularly pretty label as is often found on pure wool garments – make a feature of its 'pure wool: handwash only' tag.

Beware when felting coloured items with a white pattern: the high temperature will cause darker colours to bleed into paler ones.

Knitty Kitty

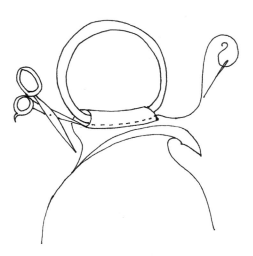

Magpie's Eye

Don't be afraid to cut knitwear up. Some garments will unravel and some will not. You will soon get the hang of it

Magpie's Eye

THE TINKER OF BIRDS, viewed with suspicion and cloaked in superstition, the magpie is a scavenger, a squatter and a thief – but never a beggar. His eye for luxury draws him to the glitzy flash of showy fortune and hungry for gilded gratification he finds himself drawn to the spinning wheels and quick change of the casino. Hopping with excitement, hypnotised by each bright new prize on offer he covets the next jewel before he's fully grasped the last so inevitably after most jaunts he flies home empty-handed. But fly home he does, for though capricious he is not fickle and never strays far from the wing of his wife. It is indeed a sorrowful day that you see him wander alone, for he never gambles with his heart, so best doff your hat in respect for it means his mate is dead. The magpie prides himself on his dress, always impeccably turned out in crisp dinner attire, white cuffs and starched collar gleaming. His black tailored suit is lined with azure satin from which are hung sapphires on silver chains, the jewels of his trade.

His erratic and flamboyant nature, the glittering heart of all-that-is-magpie, was also the root of the magpie's demise. As he did not wear full-mourning to the crucifixion, he is cursed to carry a drop of the devil's blood under his tongue. But who can begrudge a showman his flair? The blood is bitter in his throat, choking his song so that he caws like a crow. Though ashamed of his horse and gravelly voice he is eager to please and could be taught to speak words, if a patient teacher would give him the chance.

The magpie loves to accessorise, like any addict he cannot help but adorn himself with that extra hint of drama, with a brash brass pin or a bright silk scarf his is a world of carnival chaos, twinkling transience and momentary marvels. It is so clear and bright you believe the image is real but as with all sideshows, a quick flick of the black and white mediocre magician's wand, reality returns and he is gone.

Kate MacKay

Design

I was lucky to find several cotton and silk lurex-infused sweaters that were ripe for redesign and craving to be paired with other sparkly personalities. The coppery brown, emerald *chartreuse* and golden Missoni-inspired zig-zag stripes are an unexpected combination that inspires second looks. I deconstructed and redesigned them in a random sort of way with the goal of reinterpreting where parts and pieces usually appear. The deep cut back requires a tank or camisole underneath unless you are the risqué sort. This is comfy and fun to wear...sure to draw appreciative comments and stares...

Lori Marsha

TIP:
How to reshape knits

There are so many discarded woollies to be found at church fairs and charity shops. Collect ones that appeal to you due to their patterning, colour and texture. I have had a lot of fun combining patterns in interesting ways. The shape doesn't matter as you are going to reconstruct! Don't be afraid to cut the knitwear up. Some garments will unravel and some will not. You will soon get the hang of it.

One of my favourite items used in a project was a child's jumper (a largish child!) that had a fabulous elephant design knitted into the front. But the shape looked awful – it was boxy and unflattering on me.

1 Chop off a few inches from the bottom of the jersey, and re-hem it so that it finishes just above the waist. This is very flattering as it makes the waist look smaller.

2 Then cut out the sleeves and chop the curved, top part of the sleeve off in a straight line from armpit-to-armpit.

3 Turn over the top of the cut off arm pieces, and stitched down. You can now wear these pieces as gloves. The jumper now has a funky, casual flair and I feel great wearing it on the weekends with jeans.

Lori's lurex combination is very chic and original. Lurex is so glam and lends itself to elegant reconstruction – check out the way she has created an unusual a-symmetrical design.
Di Jennings

Materials

Second-hand stores, jumble sales and hand-me-downs

Knitwear in a variety of colours and patterns
Buttons, trinkets and ribbons to embellish

Craft supplies

Scissors
Needle and thread

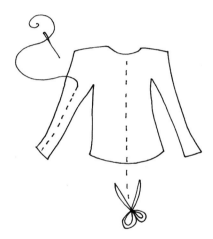

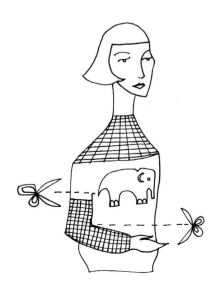

Mossy Glen
Neck Piece

❝ A great project for an old
jumper in a colour or fabric
you love, that doesn't fit ❞

Mossy Glen Neck Piece

PERHAPS IT WAS THE BEATLES who killed the collar, once such an integral and versatile style staple in the wardrobes of men and women across the demographic board. A collar can instantly transform, enhance or fetishise an outfit. It can denote rank and status and conceal unsightly neck features, be it the scarring hidden by the dazzling diamond collars of Princess Alexander of Denmark, or the lowly love bite or 'hicky' concealed beneath the well pressed school collar of many a teenager.

Collars generally fall into one of eight categories, the first is the 'Tinker': a simple square piece of cloth folded into a triangle and knotted under the chin. Originating amongst travelling folk of the Highlands, the Tinker was later adopted by cowboys of the United States who found it to be not only stylish but useful to cover their faces during raids and shootings.

Less practical but superior in craftsmanship is the 'Tailor' made famous by Shakespeare and also occasionally by singer-songwriter Björk. The Tailor is generally a quite intricately cut origami of linen which stands out from the outfit seemingly of its own accord (though in actuality aided by boning or starch). The Tailor collar was not in its day so outlandish that it couldn't be further augmented by the accompaniment of a 'Soldier' Collar. This most ornate and honorable collar was first presented to the knights of the Golden Fleece by Philip III, Duke of Burgundy; comprising of a Golden Fleece badge hung from a collar of flints, steels and sparks. A dedicated follower of fashion, Louis XI of France swiftly ordered an ornamental collar for his Order of St Michael to be made from a chain of linked scallop shells and thus the 'Soldier' Collar was born.

More often found about the necks of happy hardcore clubbers and Japanese schoolgirls, The 'Sailor' collar is a large square of fabric that fits over the head and, being detachable from the suit itself, is useful for semaphore. Usually found in navy blue with a white trim, the sailor collar is rarely worn by real sailors anymore. Those who like the Sailor collar often enjoy the Livery collar also, otherwise known as the 'Rich-Man' this collar is used to signify great wealth and status, or at least association with someone important.

Always highly precious, Rich-Man collars are unique to the wearer. Queen Anne of Bohemia wore a collar of Rosemary garnished with pearls, King Richard a White Hart and King Henry VIII a Tudor Rose. The opposite minimalist aesthetic favoured by the less flamboyant collar enthusiast may be achieved by doing away with the collar completely. A style which is derived from the Indian Kurta and made popular by The Beatles, this absence of collar is dubbed the 'Poor Man's' Collar by livery lovers.

A strap of spike encrusted leather, with a brass buckle and lead attachment was originally the garb of wolf-cautious guard dogs but now the 'Beggar Man' collar can be seen adorning the necks of submissive partners everywhere, signifying that they are owned by their other (more dominant) half. This is not to be confused with the clerical 'Priest' collar, which is white rather than black and devoid of spikes.

Kate MacKay

Design

A little bit of whimsy to wear around your neck...kind of a combination necklace/ scarf. Designed from salvaged cashmere and cotton and appliquéd in my usual funky, haphazard style. The unexpected pop of turquoise against the warm, earthy colours reminds me of Santa Fe. This one slips over your head.

Lori Marsha

TIP:

How to create a decorative collar from an old jumper

I love the way that Lori's 'collar' is part-collar part-necklace, not quite fitting either box. I like it when creations don't fit established definitions.

    This is a great project for an old jumper that you like the colour, pattern or fabric of but that doesn't fit you or complement your shape! Cotton sweatshirts are great because they won't fray; knitted jumpers can be felted beforehand if they are pure wool or the edges secured with a zig-zag stitch if they are synthetic.

1   Start by cutting the collar shape from the neck of the jumper itself. Leave a bit of room for manoeuvre, remember you can always cut off more but never less.

2   Try it on. If you like it as it is you can leave it to slip over your head, if it still looks too jumper-like you can make it smaller or wider by cutting out or inserting panels, then add buttons to do it up at the back or on the shoulder.

3   Prevent the raw edges from fraying with a zig-zag stitch.

4   Now the fun part – embellish with buttons and braids, tassels and trimmings to your heart's desire! Thinking back over the many collars I have created, there has been a lot of appliqué, using fabric scraps and off-cuts. I love working with Celtic designs, using whatever materials come my way. Incorporate the frayed edges of the woollens into your design to give it an earthy, rustic feel.

Di Jennings

Materials:

Second-hand stores, jumble sales and hand-me-downs

Jumpers in wool or cotton sweatshirts
Fabric scraps, ribbons and buttons to decorate

Craft supplies:

Needle and thread
Scissors

Chapter 5:

Heavy Duty

'It is amazing how much an
item can be transformed with
a simple button switch!'

Houndstooth Blazer

IT IS A WELL UNDERSTOOD BRITISH TRADITION that members of the fox hunt must be immaculately turned out to uphold particulars of tradition, practicality and safety. To maintain a uniform appearance on the Estate and with respect to the overall picture, the Hunt Saboteur must adhere equally to the etiquette of apparel and associated conventions.

According to the guidelines offered by the Animal Liberation Guild, the proper attire for a lady Saboteur is a tweed coat or hacking jacket, forest-coloured (jade or olive, but never white) breeches, shirt and rainbow tie or hemp shirt without collar. A stock pin, tattersall vest (no bra), vegan leather gloves, brown or black field boots and a Sab cap or safety helmet are also a must. Once a member is entitled to wear their Sabs' colours, gentlemen generally change to a scarlet coat with Sabs' colours on the collar and with brass buttons with the A.L.G insignia. Ladies wear the Sabs' colours on a black coat's collar, have the insignia on black buttons and may have black patent leather tops on their Dr Marten dress boots. Small brass buttons with the A.L.G insignia may also be worn on the waistcoat.

The most experienced and worthy Saboteurs in the eyes of the guild are awarded the honour of wearing the prestigious green houndstooth blazer. To achieve this privilege the Saboteur must have shown continued unwavering support of animals and protest skills of great daring and ingenuity both towards the hunt and towards various corporate super powers. The 'hound's tooth' name refers to the particular pattern of weave in this tweed blazer which, while attractive to the human eye, has a dizzying effect on the canine retina. When the wearer runs out in front of the hunt, the hounds become temporarily disoriented and run around in circles chasing their tails which offers ample opportunity for the fox to make his escape. If this act is performed with extreme precision and intuition it is actually possible to halt the entire hunt immediately with this single move. When this occurs it is known as a 'tooth in tail' and the houndstooth blazer-wearing Saboteur in question is awarded a floral badge of honour which she proudly stitches onto her lapel.

Kate MacKay

Design

Pursuing my favourite pastime of scouring the thrift stores, I picked up a cute, vintage cropped jacket for $3. Yes, that's right, THREE DOLLARS.

I loved the colour and the woven houndstooth design – it's fully lined as well. I didn't like the buttons; they were covered in the same material with a goldish rim around the edge. And it looks like there might have been a belt at one time, because there are little loops about 5 inches or 12½ cm up from the bottom.

As soon as I saw it, I knew what I wanted to do. I thought the hounds tooth pattern would look fun if it were appliquéd with a big, bold floral pattern – and I had some of Heather Bailey's new Pop Garden fabric which would work perfectly, the hardest part was deciding on the colour combo.

Materials

Second-hand stores, jumble sales and hand-me-downs

Vintage tweed coat
Bold floral fabric
Assorted buttons and beads

Craft supplies

Scissors
Iron
Needle and thread

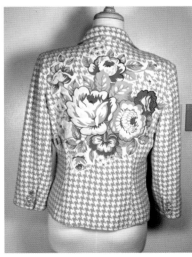

TIP:

How to add a floral motif

1   Choose a fabric with a strong floral motif. As you will be cutting out the flowers you want something with a really strong outline shape, in colours that stand out from the background jacket fabric without clashing. Probably the only way to get it right is by actually seeing it, so try laying a range of coloured motifs against your jacket; you'll know when you get the perfectly complementary combination.

2   Start with the back of the jacket. Choosing the flowers you want to add to the garment, cut out a big floral bunch in a rectangle so that there is extra fabric around the bunch of flowers.

3   Cut and iron the same size of double-sided interfacing to the piece of fabric (I use Stitch Witchery) and then cut out the floral bouquet that you want to use.

4   Position it on the back of your jacket; now you can get a clearer idea of how the motif works so when you are happy with it, pin and press it.

5   Sew it on just using a straight stitch (wrangling all those turns!). If, like mine, you find the front of your jacket could do with some colour as well, do the same with the smaller flowers in the fabric pattern.

TIP:
How to add buttons and beading

1 Once I had added my colourful blooms I could turn my attention to the button situation. I didn't like the buttons; they were covered in the same material with a goldish rim around the edge. This is often the case with vintage garments, and it is amazing how much an item can be transformed with a simple button switch!

2 After going through my stash of vintage buttons, I decided some of the beautiful rhinestone buttons I had been hoarding for years would be put to good use here. At this point, I decided to make things complicated for myself. I thought the centres of those gorgeous flowers would look extra sparkly if they were beaded. So, with no beading experience, and a complete disdain for hand sewing, I decided to add little clusters of beading...*ugh*!

3 It does look cute – it was a good idea. HOWEVER, sewing beads onto fabric that has already been interfaced and then sewn to an already heavy piece of fabric (a woven with a lining) proved very difficult.

4 If you think you'll want to add beading to a project, try to do it while the piece is still raw. I beaded all the flowers on the front and just a few on the back before I ran out of patience.

But still, I'm pretty happy with the end result! After all, it was just a $3 jacket. *Wink.*

Carrie Sommers

Skirtains

> The joy of working with ready-made curtains is the detail that has already been put into them

Skirtains

THIS MUST HAVE BEEN INFLUENCED by the emergency ensemble created by Scarlett O'Hara in *Gone With the Wind*. You have to take your hat off to the woman who freshly jilted, starving and sobbing into the curtains, has an epiphany. The next time you see her she is seducing a businessman, wearing reams of green velvet curtain, the gold fringes and tiebacks now a feature on her bonnet and handbag.

You can see by the two examples featured here how each curtain piece suggests its own character. The pencil 'skirtain' in grey blue with brass rings down the seam recalls the thrifty women at war. Whilst the tutu skirtain could have been created by the romantic servant, who *will* go to the ball! The sturdy nature and bold patterning of winter curtain fabric lends itself to strong lines and structured garments like A-line and pencil skirts. The light lace is perfect for pretty feminine garments with graceful movements and soft lines. Wear with a plain top to allow the lace details to speak volumes, or with a corset for the vintage ballerina look.

Kate MacKay

Design

As a leaving gift, a colleague at work gave me all of her mother's old curtains that she had been saving for a rainy day. Overjoyed by some of the amazing fabrics I began thinking about what I could do with them all. Thus skirtains were fashioned for my nearest and dearest.

Upholstery fabric really is of unbeatable quality, and charity shops are almost always full to the brim with incredible lengths of curtains. The lace skirtain was a real pleasure to make and I always turn heads when wearing it. It is simply made from old net curtains that have aged delightfully.

Materials: pencil skirtain

Hand-me-downs, charity shops and jumble sales

Patterned curtain with rings

Craft supplies

Sewing machine
Zip
Hook and eye
Needle and thread

Materials: tutu skirtain

Hand-me-downs, charity shops and jumble sales

Net curtains
Curtain tacking – rolls can often be found in charity shops as fewer people make their own curtains, or you can un-pick tacking from existing old curtains.

Craft supplies

Sewing machine
Hook and eye
Needle and thread

TIP:
How to make a pencil skirtain

The joy of working with ready-made curtains is the detail that has already been put into them. For example, this pencil skirt had curtain rings built into the fabric. I simply slipped the fabric onto its side so that the rings became a feature at the back – not quite a fishtail and not quite a corset, but eye-catching none the less. The weighty fabric is perfect for giving you a strong silhouette and for hugging the figure in all the right places.

As each individual curtain will vary, experiment by holding it against you in a variety of ways. Think about how the fabric will hang and consider which features can enhance the waist band, seam and hem.

1 Place the top edge according to the kind of waist you would like, ours has a high waistline but hipsters are very sexy too, whatever suits you best.

2 When you are happy with the design cut to the length you desire and give some space for seam allowance at the back, or overlap like we've done here.

3 Run a straight stitch up the back to hold it together. You may need to double this up to ensure that seams don't burst while you're on the dance floor! Because of the interesting curtain ring feature I didn't even need to create a seam, it's best to try and enhance the qualities of the piece of fabric you have found; this is where being creative with recycling offers the opportunity to break the mould.

4 As the fit is so tight leave plenty of room for a long zip to enable you to get in and out of the dress without difficulty. Or if you are daring, have a zip all the way down so you can vary how much you reveal. Add a button, ribbon or hook and eye at the top to secure the zip.

5 If you want to make a high-waister skirt you will need to insert 8 darts, 4 front and 4 back to give the shape. A hipster is fine left as it is.

a ribbon to the tacking to fasten the skirt and you're ready to go.

4 Experiment with doubling up and layering the net curtains; each garment will be individual depending on the fabric you find. Lining may be used as well, since the net is largely transparent. Why not try a bright colour for contrast and to really emphasise the design on your lace?

TIP:
How to make a tutu skirtain

Curtain tacking is a great basis for a waistband; it has a strong structure and loops already in place to attach fastenings to. You can make it a feature or hide it behind fabric as I have done here.

1 Measure the curtain tacking so it is the same size as your waist. Pin your net curtain to the waist band, folding the fabric into concertina 'knife pleats' as you go.

2 This net fabric has a beautiful spear-like shape that finishes the skirt off perfectly, giving it great movement; try to keep ideas about how it is finished at the edges in mind, as this will really affect your overall design. Sew this on using a straight running stitch.

3 Sew the edges of the skirt together, making sure you leave enough room to step into it. When stitching the lace together it is important to use a small zig-zag stitch and to follow the main line of design. Sew a hook and eye, a button or

Consider which features can enhance the waist band, seam and hem

165

Inner Tube Necklace

My inner tube necklace
combines my love of cycling
and recycling!

Inner Tube Necklace

IN 1822, BARON KARL VON DRAIS of Mannheim, Germany, invented the dandy horse (or '*Laufmaschine*' as Drais called it). Although the dandy horse is to the modern bicycle what the great apes are to the modern man, in Germany in the 19th century they were considered a modern marvel. If you owned a dandy horse, you had 'made it'. You were the kind of chap the guys wanted, and the girls wanted to be.

The dandy horse was the bike for the utilitarian, unlike those of today, where technical wizardry allows the rider to cheat an incline or safely slow on a corner. *Ney*! Pedals, breaks and gears and other such witchcraft were considered by the purists as frivolities and extravagances. Although the design may not have been friendly to the anatomy of the male gender, impotence was a small price to pay for the adulation and praise one received for owning a dandy horse. Although modern bicycles have evolved greater complexities, the dandy horse was still the favoured method of transport for the fashionable gent about town and dare devil actor Buster Keaton, who rode one in the film *Our Hospitality* (1923). In fact, Buster was heard to have once said, 'I really like my dandy horse, it is dead good.' If Buster was alive today he would be riding a dandy horse right now.

In 1846, a young, humble Scottish inventor named Robert William Thomson, invented the pneumatic tyre. Forty-three years later, fellow Scot John Boyd Dunlop, incorporated it into a tricycle design for his son. From this came Dunlop's invention of the modern bicycle. Dunlop also claimed to be the inventor of the pneumatic tyre and was granted its patent, despite the true inventor being Thomson. Thomson was an old man by this time, but still armed with a spine of solid steel and a mind as sharp as a sabre's point. He rightfully disputed Dunlop's claim. Two years later, the battle was finally resolved in a bike race of Herculean proportions. Thomson challenged Dunlop to a thousand-mile bike race, from Cape Wrath in Scotland to Land's End in Cornwall. The first to cross the finishing line would win the patent to the pneumatic tyre.

On the morning of the race, the public arrived at Cape Wrath to witness what was destined to be the greatest competition since Ajax and Odysseus battled for Achilles' armour. The young Dunlop stood confidently in front of his modern bicycle fitted out with pneumatic tyres, brakes and a suede-lined saddle. Whilst

the sixty-three-year-old, white-haired Thomson, refusing to use Dunlop's bicycle invention, quietly wheeled up his steel wheeled dandy horse. It seemed to all that the old man with an antique machine could never compete against Dunlop's modern design and youthful physique. However, this was a case of David and Goliath, where heart counted more than modern invention. Sixteen days later Thomson reached Cornwall, a full three days before Dunlop. Dunlop was so moved by the old man's grit, that he made a public apology to Thomson, offering over the patent. As a symbolic gesture of respect, Thomson made a garland from his own bike's inner tubes. To this day, every year the same 'Thomson Dandy Horse' race is run, with the winner receiving a small cut square from the inner tube of each competitor, in memory of Thomson, 'a tough old dog who rode a dandy horse'.
Will Brownlie is a writer and biologist based in Edinburgh

Design

My inner tube necklace combines my love of cycling and recycling! Add to this the satisfaction in creating something beautiful from the mundane. This readily accessible and free source material would otherwise be thrown out, so your local bike shop will be grateful for the extra bin space.

The resulting tactile creation is surprisingly wearable and comfortable: warming up nicely. It was my first ever sale at my first ever craft market.

Using the valve as a clasp is a fitting homage to the material's source. Everything is sacred!

My wonderfully inspirational friend Naomi described a necklace she saw in Paris made from a piece of ornately-cut rubber decorated with beads which we tried in vain to replicate. Surrounded by strips of tubing I later attempted a *lei*-style garland which ultimately evolved into this item: a happy accident.

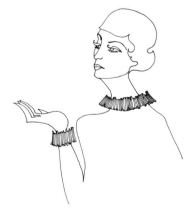

My local bike shop was more than happy to donate its defunct inner tubes to me (much to the curiosity of the staff). These were otherwise destined for landfill.

The necklace almost looks like it's made from slate. Apologetic strangers frequently ask to touch it!
Knitty Kitty

Materials

Bike shop

2-3 bicycle inner tubes
(depending on the length of the
necklace)

Craft supplies

Sharp scissors
Awl (leather hole punch) or good
quality paper hole punch
Heavy duty elastic
Tapestry/darning needle
Washing facility for cleaning
inner tube
A comfortable seat and a
degree of patience

TIP:

How to make an inner tube necklace

1   Kindly ask your local bike shop for 2-3 defunct inner tubes from their bin (it may be necessary to field off questions as to your intention with these grubby rubber innards!).

2   Some tubes are heavier than others, if you have a choice opt for a more lightweight tube.

3   Using a sharp pair of scissors, cut each tube into thirds, lengthwise. This may vary depending on the breadth of the tyre or how chunky you want your squares to be. Ultimately the thickness of your first lengthwise cuts will determine the size of the finished squares.

4   Wash and dry the tubes.

5   Make yourself comfortable, the next task is repetitive and time-consuming!

6   Further cut the long strips into equal-sized squares of 1 inch (25mm).

7   Line the squares up according to the direction of the tyre's curve so each square fits snugly behind the next like so: ((((

8   Using the awl or hole punch at its largest setting, make a hole central to each square. Again, maintain the curved shape of the tyre to save time when threading together.

9   Repeat ad nauseum!

10 With the punched squares lined up, you can gauge how many more you need to cut and decide what size of necklace/bracelet you wish to make. Bear in mind that the longer the piece, the heavier it will be. When you have reached your desired length, thread a darning/tapestry needle with heavy duty elastic (necessary to support the weight).

11 Now thread the squares together with the curves facing the same direction.

12 When you have reached the length you require, you can simply knot the elastic to secure it.

13 Alternatively, as I have done, you can use the tyre's valve to finish the piece. This requires a pair of pliers to hollow out the valve by removing the inner mechanism: you need to be able to thread the elastic through. It also serves as a clever means of hiding the bulky knot (you want to keep all that hard work well secured!).

Bracelets require part of one inner tube and may serve as a good starting point.

14 To break up the monotony of a solid string of squares, you can always add curiosities in the form of bike workings/ mechanisms: i.e. small cogs. I have also contemplated using parts of bike pumps to add character and colour to the necklace. On the other hand, the uniformity of the piece is a large part of its appeal.

• Variation: for a more authentic *lei*-style piece, cut the tubes into random shapes.

• Things to consider: an awl (adjustable-size leather hole punch) is a worthwhile and relatively inexpensive craft investment. Only yesterday, I 'brogue-ified' a pair of shoes: using said awl to create flower patterns in a pair of shoes, freshly purchased from my local Salvation Army charity shop, in my eternal quest for a pair of grown-up sized pair of children's shoes – ankle strap *et al*! It can also be used as an alternative to an eyelet maker, to ease the task of stitching/ lacing together of heavy duty fabrics.

Knitty Kitty

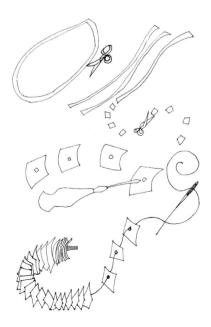

Scottish Lassie

‘Our Scottish Lassie is gorgeous
but in no way traditional.
The pièce de résistance: three
ring binders attached to the
shoulder for 'bagpipes' ’

Scottish Lassie

THE TARTAN KILT is the formal attire still favoured at Scottish weddings, graduations, awards ceremonies, rugby matches and Ceilidhs. The gentleman's kilt remains ever-popular, giving as it does the freedom and flexibility required for sword dancing, the strength and durability for whisky-fuelled battle and endless comic japes that can be played on or by the wearer of what is essentially a man-skirt.

The kilt was originally one big piece of fabric woven in a tartan particular to the clan. It would be held in place entirely by a complicated system of pleating and knotting, somewhat like an Indian sari. The kilt was especially handy when clans were making the long march into battle as at night the fabric would double up as a shelter, could be made into a flag to rally the troops or the strong weave of the cloth could even be used to filter water for drinking when supplies were low.

Such a versatile and practical garment was necessary as it was not uncommon for the men to take huge detours when on a march, in the hope of discovering the lost Clan of Cape Wrath.

The Clan of Cape Wrath was said to be a nomadic matriarchy, comprised entirely of women famed for their promiscuity and battle skills. They were the only women to wear kilts and the only people to wear the tartan of another clan. These 'she-kilts' (irreverent in so many ways), were a sight to behold; pinned together with thorns they were a veritable rainbow of tartan patches. After spending a night with a member of Cape Wrath a man could expect to find an empty bed and a patch torn out of his kilt. These were pinned onto the she-kilt as trophies of all the men they had 'conquered'. Our Scottish Lassie is an example of quite a new young member of Cape Wrath which is why her patchwork tartan skirt is still so short. In a few years it would probably be trailing along behind her.

Kate MacKay

Design

Three years spent living in beautiful Edinburgh, Scotland, inspired me to create our wee Scottish Lassie. She is gorgeous but in no way traditional. Her outfit is made from an eclectic mix of materials including a lace shawl, tartan fabric scraps, a woven belt and a tartan purse. The *pièce de résistance* has to be the three ring binders attached to the shoulder to look like bagpipes! The beret is crocheted from red and black plastic shopping bags and finished with a pom-pom made from onion bags!

Di Jennings

Materials: sporran

Hand-me-downs, charity shops and jumble sales

Woven belt
Tartan purse
Beaded bracelet
Lace shawl off-cuts (for tassels)

Materials: shoulder sash

Hand-me-downs, charity shops and jumble sales

Military-style epaulette
3 black ring binders
Tartan fabric/scraps
Fine black woven belt
Black lace scrap
Bead or bauble (for the centre of the rosette)

Craft supplies

Needle and thread

TIP:
How to make the 'sporran'

1   I gathered the above materials from scrap stores and charity shops. The African bangle looked great hand sewn to the front of the wee tartan purse.

2   Half of a square lace scarf was left over from the main part of the costume and the sporran needed some tassels so I cut the scarf about ⅓ inch (1 cm) above the line where the tassels met the lace, divided it into two lengths and tightly rolled each piece into a tassel.

3   To hold the top part of the tassel I wound around many circles of thread and fastened this in place and then hand stitched the tassels to the bottom of purse.

4   The purse has fine black straps that I wove through the strands of the red belt and hand stitched firmly in place.

It is not intended that you duplicate any of these ideas exactly. Our aim is to show you what can be done creatively with found objects and throw-away bits and bobs. Look around at the waste and excess objects in your environment that inspire you and get creative!

For inspiration, look around at the waste and excess objects in your environment

TIP:

How to make the shoulder sash

1   I found the elements required in my assembled 'sea of stuff' and started to play with them. I had a number of strips of tartan fabric that were long enough to drape across the body and create a sash at back and front. One was narrower than the other – so I decided to attach the narrower piece to the wider piece to create a layered effect. As I stitched the top piece I made some tucks in the middle section that added some depth to create a military effect that looks like cases for storing bullets.

2   Then I added a third layer by hand sewing the narrow leather belt to the centre running from the shoulder to the hip.

3   I glued the epaulette in place on the shoulder with hot glue and carefully attached the three ring binders. Placing them to look like bagpipes was initially challenging and required some persistence, but I got there in the end with a combination of hand stitching and gluing.

4   I joined the ends of the tartan sash at the hip, leaving about 20 inches (50cm) to form a side train. The sash still looked unfinished so I decided to make a rosette to complete the effect.

5   For the rosette. I used a tartan scrap, folded it in half, pressed along the fold and then gathered up the raw edge and joined the short ends to create a circle. I had a scrap of lace left over from the shawl and repeated the process with the lace to form a smaller circle. Then I placed the small lace circle in the middle of the larger tartan one and hand stitched this in the middle. It still needed a centre so I used a large glass bead to complete the rosette and then hand stitched the rosette to the sash at the hip. The entire sash was then hand sewn to the lace shawl to create an a-symmetrical effect.

Di Jennings

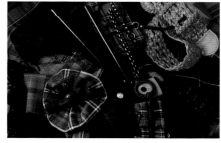

Tiny Tartan **Tote**

❝A simple, easily-recognisable shape as the basis for a pretty, safe-keeping keepsake❞

Tiny Tartan Tote

A FASHION ACCESSORY can be defined as a decorative item that enhances one's outfit. A brooch, a neckerchief, gloves, a pith helmet; all of these items used correctly can make wonderful fashionable side dishes. If I said, 'I like your brooch, but have you thought of enhancing your outfit with a matching live animal?', I am sure you would look at the floor awkwardly, shifting your weight from foot to foot and mumble that I was crazy 'as a minnow at a heron's tea party'. I would agree with you.

Such a proposition is surely ludicrous, but even as we speak, young heiresses and two-dimensional socialites are using the common lap dog as such a device. The Pomeranian, or Pompom dog, is frequently a supplement to an evening's outfit; a fashion add-on; a patronised side salad of a spoilt main course. These poor little creatures are further cheapened with their own accessories, usually co-ordinated with their owners'. Diamanté collars, manicures and designer haircuts are commonplace. I once witnessed a Pekinese in stilettos.

In my research for this article I was contacted by a Shih-Tzu who wishes to remain anonymous. He told me how he had once been made to wear a tutu (commercially known as a Shih-Tzu-tu) and on another occasion was made to wear a suit of armour, demeaned by the name 'Sir Pups-alot' for the duration of this nightmarish evening. When a lap dog is accessorised, the world must ask if accessorising has gone too far? The newest of crazes is adorning a lap dog with its own lap dog, known in the trade as 'Russian Dolling it Pup'. Will we soon be able to buy fashion accessories for the fleas that live on the lap dogs of the lap dogs? When will it ever end? The sad answer is almost maybe definitely never.

Genetic studies show that the earliest breeds of domestic dog were the Pekinese lapdog. These little chaps were bred in ancient China and lived in the sleeves of unsuspecting Chinese dignitaries of the Imperial Palace. Although they could be smoked out or tempted out using various meat products, they were for most part a welcome guest. They provided purpose, providing warmth as well as guarding against ring thieves.

Although in general dogs have served as the favourite lap animal, other species have been employed with varying success. The Egyptians used cats and lizards, the Norwegian's accessorised with hedgehogs and the Turkish originally

used small cows but found this impractical, later preferring dwarf goats adorned with ornate jewel-encrusted clogs. In Scotland, the animal of choice was the partridge. This ritual is all but lost, although it is still occasionally witnessed in some of the Hebridean Islands to the North. The partridge was dressed to match the clan's tartan and carried under the left oxter (arm-pit), viewed as a sign of propriety. We believe the elegance of carrying a live partridge can be equalled by making a model, such as the ones featured in this 'ere book. This is fairer to animals and has the distinct advantage of avoiding the embarrassment of a defecating partridge whilst hob-knobbing with the hoi polloi.
Will Brownlie

Design

Hawk haggis hybrid holdall! Tiny tartan tote for travelling twitchers!

This is made using a very simple, easily-recognisable shape as the basis for a pretty safe-keeping keepsake. Being based in Scotland is advantageous for easy access to tartan scraps but any small remnant will suffice for this project. I have a ream of tartan left over after altering a floor-length kilt into a mini version, which will give rise to a flock of purses. Maybe I should look into giving them Clan names… The key is to keep the shape simple: let the patterned fabric speak for itself. I hope to branch out into other critters soon and maybe even do some imaginary creatures.

I am inspired by ornithology, tartan and buttons – especially the leather-covered buttons that are frequently found on Aran cardigans. Where possible, these are the eyes I give my birds. I have a hooded Aran cardigan my mother made me when I was about eight years old that I still try and squeeze myself into, adorned with these beloved buttons.

Initially these purses started life as a tampon-holder: having noticed a huge gap in the market for said storage devices. My beloved bird can also house my portable techy tools: USB sticks, SD card reader and adaptors. Although I do also have a pretty floral version for girlier gadgets!
Knitty Kitty

Materials

Hand-me-downs, charity shops and jumble sales

2 small scraps fabric, approximately 8 inches x 5 inches (20cm x 12cm)
2 buttons – leather-covered or otherwise

Craft supplies

1 x 4 inches (10cm) closed end zip
Sewing equipment: sewing machine if available, dressmaker's chalk, needle and thread, pins, scissors
Cardboard or baking parchment and a pencil to create the template
An iron

TIP:
How to make a bird purse

1   Draw a simple bird shape onto a piece of cardboard, using the illustration on p.183 as a guide. Cut this out to use as a template.

2   Pin 2 pieces of fabric 'right' sides together.

3   Using dressmaker's chalk, draw around the template onto the fabric.

4   Hand or machine stitch around chalked shape leaving an opening at the top of approximately 4 ⅓ inches (11cm) for your zip, and maintaining a ⅕ inch (½cm) seam allowance. This can be trimmed down at the final stage.

5   Turn the bird inside-out so the 'right' side faces out and the seams are on the inside.

6   Now iron the shape to flatten down the seams – rounding the curves of the bird's belly and sharpening the beak. Use your fingers to poke the seam to the edge before pressing.

7   Line the zip up with the opening – the closed/bottom end of the zip should sit at the tip of the bird's 'tail' so the small excess at the end of the zip can be tucked and caught inside the purse.

8   Pin the wrong side of the zip to right side of one layer of the purse: the bird's 'back' as it were. This will require some figuring out: when the zip is flipped to the right side facing up, the seam allowance of the bird's back will sit on the inside. The excess at the top of the zip should sit along the inside of the stitched 'head'.

9   Repeat for the other side. Ensure that when the zip is closed, it sits flatly and evenly.

10   For such a small zip and if you are not adept at the fine art of zip insertion, it is advisable to hand stitch this part. You have greater control and it is easy to stitch a straight line as close to the zip's teeth as possible, without affecting the smooth running of the zip.

11 If you are confident with zips and have a sewing machine, use a zipper foot to stitch the zip close to the teeth.

12 Also attach the start and end of the zip to the top and bottom of the opening to keep it secure and neat.

13 Turn inside-out and trim the excess seams. Also cut the seam poking out from under the zip so it cannot be seen. Very carefully, top stitch the zip to the side of the bird. This means creating a row of stitches to hold the zip flatly down by very lightly hooking a few threads from the side of the bird but not enough that it can be seen.

14 Finally, your reward for finicky zip fixing – sew an eye on each of the bird's sides! I love this moment of granting each creature real character the moment you attach the buttons. You will be surprised at the different personalities you can grant your winged wonder with the placement or type of button you choose.

An Irish tradition if giving a purse is to put in a small coin or Doubloon.
Knitty Kitty

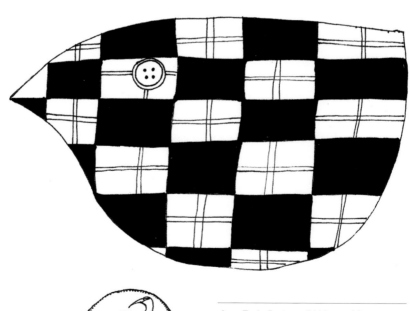

An Irish tradition if giving a present of a purse is to put in a small coin or Doubloon

Chapter 6:

Paper

'This has gotten the single
best reaction of anything I
have made... it's the ultimate
party hat!'

Hat O'Cards

WHAT WOULD YOU SAY if I screeched the following words to you in a very high voice, like a ruddy-faced drill sergeant: 'The plug, the topper, the silk, the stove pipe, the chimney pot, the fancy man'?

Why, you would exclaim in a justified panic, 'What?! Why are you shouting these random words at me, and in such an unruly order? Bally-hell man, what on earth are you playing at? Who the devil do you think you are?'

With a glitter in my eye and a skip in my heel, I would lean a little closer and relieve you of your terrified panic. 'I am not a madman on the loose who is trying to steal your outer garments and neckerchief with jive talk, ney no! I tell you, these words are connected. Please kind sir, take these phrases and place the word "hat" after each one and all will become clear. Yes, you see? They are all names that have been used to describe the top hat. Phew!'

The top hat is my favourite of all hats. Garnish my head with one! Proud and tall, may it stand true like a soot-covered ivory tower of elegance. Now, tilt it to a roguish angle of seven degrees and there you have it, you have immediately transformed me: from hedge sparrow to peacock; from sessile barnacle to thrashing skip-jack tuna; a timid dormouse to a not-so-timid door knocker. If you wear a top hat, you are making a statement that reads: 'I am a man of distinction; breathe in the cooling winds of my infinite style, for I am "a someone" indeed!'

The best top hats were made of felted beaver fur. For gentlemen on a budget, rabbit pelt was used and for the destitute a rat on a stick would make-do. Mercury was used in the felt-making process. The dangers associated with inhaling mercury fumes are extreme: if you inhale mercury it causes neurological damage. As a result eleven out of ten master hat makers suffered from utter lunacy, giving rise to the phrase 'as mad as a hatter'.

Mercury not only causes neurodegenerative disorders, it is also corrosive. The hats worn by traditional hat makers showed this, displaying holes and rips in weakened felts from long-term exposure to these noxious fumes. A colourful fashion was adopted when holes were fixed with a playing card. One could tell the length of a hat maker's career, and therefore their level of experience, by the number of cards patching up their hat. This soon became the formal statement of hierarchy. The contentious shopper would not wish to buy from any hat maker who had less than ten cards fixed to their hat. A master hat maker would wear a hat almost completely made of cards, but due to such a length of service, these fellows were usually completely mad. This metric was embraced by all but the most rapscallion hat makers.

In 1867, Jacques de la Marque made the discovery that mercury was a mind-addling agent and after a lengthy court battle it was outlawed immediately. To this day mercury is still illegal; only the Queen is allowed to own it, keeping it in a large bottle in her castle.

Even though mercury is no longer used to make hats, these fine traditions and eccentricities still live on. To this day when a hat maker reaches the level of master, he is presented with the ceremonial card top hat, recognising the fine pioneer mad hatters of the past.

Will Brownlie

Design

Looking for an inspiring idea of what to do with accumulated, incomplete packs of playing cards, I found this wonderful idea made by Sergey Chernyshev on the Instructables website (see www.instructables.com/id/Party-top-hat-made-of-playing-cards).

It has gotten the single best reaction of anything I have made, from commenting passers-by to requests from friends who want to borrow it. Sergey and I both have a propensity to collect playing cards. They are a staple of both charity shops and jumble sales: with a wide range of styles available, from beautifully ornate designs to cheesy tourist souvenirs!

You can choose whether to have the actual playing card face or the patterned backs on display. Either way it makes the ultimate party hat!

Last Christmas, my family's crackers yielded a pack of miniature playing cards which I took great delight in fashioning into a post-turkey festive accessory.
Knitty Kit

TIP:
How to make a hat from cards

Materials

Second-hand stores and hand-me-downs

Approximately 2 packs playing cards

Craft supplies

Stapler and staples
Ruler
Pliers/staple remover
P.V.A. glue (optional)

Top of hat:

1 To make the top of the hat, attach cards in a line – long sides together. Staple two cards, overlapping them just enough for one staple, with the cards angled slightly towards a narrow 'ventilation' hole in the centre. Check to see if you have stapled through both cards.

2 Keep stapling them to make a line of cards (the amount of cards depends on your head size; for example my head measures 22 inches (53cm) just above the eyebrow, which called for thirteen cards).

3 Staple the last card to first one and try it on your head – it should fit relatively tightly. You may need to add or subtract a card or shift several cards a little to adjust more precisely. A staple remover can save your nails!

4 Next, remove one staple to return it back to flat form.

5 Then get a ruler and use it to bend an edge of the cards up. It doesn't really matter how much you leave for bending, it will only affect the size of the ventilation hole in the middle.

6 Now, when you bend the whole thing to form a plate shape, you can connect the last and first cards together to see how it will look.

Body of hat:

1 To attach the body of the hat, remove one staple again and attach a card face to the face of the folded top: shorter sides together with 'wrong' (inside) sides facing.

2 Keep stapling until you get the whole circle of lengthwise cards finished.

The whole project takes about an hour, or two when you do it for the first time

3 To add some height, attach more rows if you want. It doesn't matter actually how many rows you put or whether you attach long or short sides of cards. You can also shift the next row along against the previous one to make the pattern more interesting. Feel free to improvise! You can either use one row of staples or do a double row.

4 When you're finished the second row, attach it to make a cylinder. It'll be much harder to do when you have a third row (depending on the size of your stapler).

5 Now try it on and make sure it fits – it's still not too late to adjust the size, you can do this up until you make the brim.

6 Next, staple the top cards leaving a small ventilation hole on top. (Although you can do this later it'll make the structure stronger and will help you with handling the hat at later stages if you do it now.)

7 A very small stapler makes this next task easier but it's possible with a large one too: just staple through the cards; the more staples, the stronger the hat.

Brim of hat:

1 Now you have to make a supporting row linking the body of the hat and the brim. Staple some cards that match the bottom colour of the brim facing into the hat, overlapping the sides, with half of the length of the card sticking out below the body of the base.

2 Then cut the sticking-out cards in half with scissors and bend them out so they spread out evenly. You can probably cut them into three parts to make an edge

more round and smooth but you'll have to do more stapling later and that's a lot of staples. Try your hat on one last time to make sure that it fits perfectly – after this step you will not be able to change anything without unstapling the whole thing.

3 Next attach the top layer of cards for the brim by stapling them to the folded out 'half-cards' you made in the last step. Make sure they are aligned evenly/radially and not skewed left or right. Overlap cards to cover about ½ to ⅔ of the previous card – you need relatively smooth edges to the brim. Be aware that the brim takes most of the cards and it can make the hat heavier if you overlap too much, or less strong and neat if you overlap too little.

Also make sure you staple through the cards on the bottom – this will give the brim its necessary strength. You might want to shape it into an oval to match the form of your head.

4 Now align a card on the bottom layer to match the top level and staple the cards close to the outer edge. Here you might want to use pliers or something similar to flatten the staples so they don't bother you much when you touch them.

Finishing touches:

When you've finished attaching all the cards (remember, the last card should go under the first one), do another round of stapling closest to the sides of the cylinder making sure that the flat sides of staples are towards the bottom of the hat – otherwise the ends of the staples will give your hair a hard time.

Voila! You can put a joker or one of the aces sticking out of the top of the hat for added effect.

A layer of P.V.A. glue painted over the outside will give a nice overall sheen.
From an original idea by Sergey Chernyshev, interpreted by Catherine Walsh, in a cross-continent collaboration

P.V.A. glue painted over the outside of the hat will give a nice overall sheen

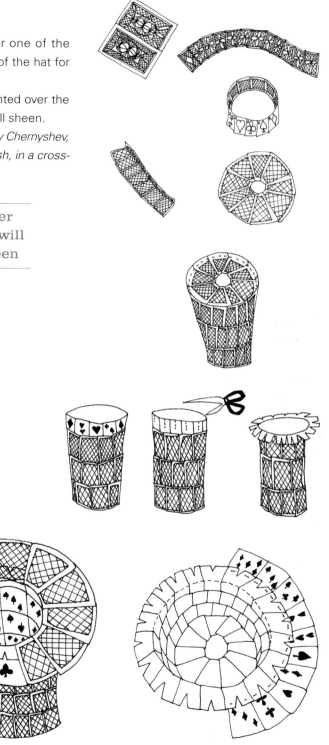

Paper Beads

‘ This cheerful necklace is made from the glossy pages of free promotional magazines ’

Paper Beads

THE ART OF BEADING is central to traditional North American culture. Assorted elements were collected from the environment, methodically manipulated, transformed into beautiful and precious objects and attire through a process that was both social and ceremonial. The value in the beaded artworks resides not in the scarcity of their components, but in the respectful artistry with which the natural elements have been transformed. Porcupine quills were collected and dyed, soaked and sewn with their own natural porcupine needle point into birch bark and tanned hide. Bold geometric designs, the natural curves of flowers and trees were painstakingly woven with individual porcupine quills to create artworks magnificent to behold. With the European settlers came the glass seed bead and the ancient art of porcupine quilling was largely lost.

It is said that there is one ancient woman who still practices the art but nobody's memory stretches far enough to remember where she is and all the roads have yet to find her. In her hidden cave she sits; untouched and unaware of the changes brought by the settlers, patiently working on quilling her magnificent buffalo robe. Her face is shrivelled like a walnut, her eyes faded like sunken pebbles and her teeth are worn to little stumps, she has used them to flatten so many porcupine quills. Resting beside her is Shunka Sapa, a huge black dog contentedly licking his lips and watching her every move. Every time the old woman painfully hobbles over to stir the *wojapi* that is forever boiling over on the fire she has kept lit for a thousand years or more, the huge black dog leaps up and pulls all the porcupine quills out from the Buffalo Robe. Eternally the woman returns to continue her never-ending task. For according to the Sioux, the huge black dog knows that at the very moment the old woman threads the last porcupine quill and completes her design the world will come to an end.

Kate MacKay

Design

The materials are sourced from my own collection, from donations, swaps, thrift shops, online auction sites and from a shop called Bits and Bobs – a recycled material supplier run by volunteers in Edinburgh. The reason why I create a diverse range of applied artwork relates to the scarcity of certain materials that I favour. This means I can keep working until new and curious materials present themselves.

This cheerful necklace is made from pages taken from free promotional magazines. I liked the colours and the glossy surface and printed numbers and slogans. In this piece I have made different sized beads and threaded them together with matching bright yellow glass beads and plastic buttons.

Sarah Galliers

TIP:

How to make glossy paper beads

1 Choose a vivid glossy magazine, select pages that attract you through their colour and design. Fold the page into four lengthways. Draw a long triangular shape from the top, 1¼ inch (3cm) approximately at top and ¼ inch (7mm) at bottom.

2 Cut out four triangle shapes. Take one triangle shape at a time and paste water based glue on one side.

3 With a darning needle or knitting needle slowly roll the strip towards you starting with the widest edge. (Make sure the bead moves freely on the needle.) Keep rolling all the way and smooth down the narrow end.

4 Leave to dry.

5 Experiment with the effects different triangles have on the end bead shape, slightly a-symmetrical triangles can have an unusual less uniform effect, the chunky, rounder beads in this example were achieved by using several triangular strips of descending size.

6 Use water-based glue to varnish the outsides of the beads, this will make them last longer as they will be a bit more study. You can embellish them further with glitter and sequins as I have done here.

7 Once dry you are ready to pin, thread or sew the beads into your work – the possibilities are endless!

Sarah Galliers

Materials

Your recycling

Assortment of glossy magazines or wrapping paper

Craft supplies

Scissors
Darning or knitting needle
Water-based glue

Use water-based glue to varnish the beads and make them last longer

Carnival Time

‘ Made from hundreds of
out-of-date flyers collected
from the local council,
our "Madame Eco" celebrates
building communities at a
neighbourhood level ’

Carnival Time

THE *COMMEDIA DELL'ARTE* was the theatrical origin of many themes and characters we are now so familiar with; revolving around the brash heartless harlequin and the gentle melancholic Pierrot and their quest for the love of the fair Columbine. While Harlequin famously later became the iconic Mr Punch – that loveable rogue popular at the British seaside – less is known about the origins of Punch's long-suffering wife Judy.

Some look for clues in a dubious warm-up act which preceded the original *Commedia*, comprising of a mysterious woman weaving her way through the crowd. Her face was masked and she walked solemnly, dressed in a crinoline made from envelopes. From the hem to the bodice, every frill, pleat and hooped underskirt was an envelope, said to contain messages from the 'other side'. Known as Madame Scribe, she was feared and revered and in her prime proved much more popular than the *Commedia* itself. The other actors couldn't stand her. As a warm-up act she was terrible, by the time the house lights went up on the main show most of the audience would be overcome with grief.

This did not concern Madame Scribe, who considered herself to be the true attraction and the others to be merely side show acts. Her arrogance was eventually her demise. Rumour had it that she was becoming careless, she was often late, her act was shabby and she had even started keeping tobacco and snacks in a few of the pockets, smoking and stuffing her face between acts. Eventually the inevitable happened. A man stepped forward from the hushed crowd, with eyes full of loss, his trembling hands reached in despair for a fragment of the past and he pulled out a nibbled piece of ham. A moment of disbelief and the hordes were in hysterics. Madame Scribe became Judy, the domestic-abuse-suffering puppet-wife of Mr Punch, doomed to perpetually pull strings of sausages from her knickers. The legacy of her arrogance is that, to this day, to act in a manner unconvincing to your audience is termed 'to ham it up'.
Kate MacKay

Design

I adore watching costume dramas. The beauty of the clothes and sets has just as much attraction for me as the enjoyment of the drama. Madame Eco-llaboration takes us back to Madame Pompadour and the court of Louis XV.

My colleague Kim and I were working together in the Waitakere community in Auckland, New Zealand when we both became inspired to create Madame Eco-llaboration. My work focus at the time was community collaboration and Kim was working on an environmental project. We decided to get together to create an entry into the Waitakere Trash to Fashion Awards that reflected our combined interests in an exciting and innovative way.

Madame Eco-llaboration is mainly made from discarded community flyers. For the base of the dress, we found a discarded roll of cardboard that was backed by bubble wrap at the local tip. It was just the right weight to create the bell-shaped skirt and bodice that we hand stitched together. When working on a large piece like this, I like to work on each piece separately – so although in the photo it looks like one dress it is actually a separate skirt and bodice and the sleeves are also separate. Having established the basic shape we started playing with the flyers we had collected, arranging them into patterns, and then pasted/ glued them onto our base shapes. We also added photographs of some of the

movers and shakers in our community into the mix. It was fun watching them find themselves peeping out from the skirts of Madame E (as she affectionately became named in our community). The mask is made of *papier-mâché* and the gravity-defying headdress emerged when we gathered an old mosquito net over a cane stool – and added recycled paper ringlets for a final touch!

*by Di Jennings, Kim Morresey
and friends*

Materials: collage

Your recycling

Discarded flyers

Craft supplies

Blu-Tack
Glue gun
Craft paste

Materials: mask

Second-hand

A plaster head or similar
to use as a mould

Your recycling

Newspaper

Craft supplies

Vaseline
Flour and water
Paint

TIP:
How to collage using discarded flyers

1 Collect hundreds of out-of-date flyers from community groups and the local council. We chose flyers that had an immediate appeal in terms of their colour, pattern or design.

2 Play with the flyers – sort them into pleasing colour combinations and try creating different shapes. Experiment! Place into circles, ovals and fans. You will know when you have made a pleasing formation. We particularly enjoyed making fan shapes.

3 Glue or staple the flyers together and arrange them onto your base garment. Our design is quite elaborate, but you could create a very simple shape. A simple A-line frock could look very cool and 1960s. Take your time.

4 Use Blu-Tack to attach the flyers temporarily as you shift them around. We found that craft paste worked well to attach the lightweight fliers, but the heavier weight formations needed a hot glue gun to hold them in place.

5 Fill in gaps between formations with neutral colours. We used old maps – this looked just right and provided a sense of place or neighbourhood. This was perfect as the work that Mme E celebrates is all about building communities at a neighbourhood level.

> Use Blu-Tack to attach the flyers temporarily as you shift them around

TIP:

How to make the *papier-mâché* mask

I have always loved masks. They enable an immediate transformation into another persona. Masquerades provide us with permission to play out fantasies and experiment with being a different character for a while. When I visited Venice I was captivated with the ornate, beautiful masks that are made for the annual carnival in February. I understand that historically this practice of wearing a mask for courting lead to some very decadent behaviour at times! Undoubtedly wearing a mask creates an alluring air of mystery and intrigue.

I decided to create a mask for Madame E as make-up at the time of Madame Pomopadour was so heavy that it created the impression of a mask being worn. I often find that techniques I have not tried seem difficult until I have a go – and then I am surprised at how easy it can be once you begin. I had not worked with *papier-mâché* before and was pleased at how simple it was to create this mask for Mme E.

1   I used an old plaster head as a mould and cut up newspaper into small pieces.

2   Then I made a glue from flour and water and stirred in the torn up newspaper to make the *papier-mâché* mixture.

3   Before applying the *papier-mâché*, I smeared the face of the plaster head with Vaseline to prevent the first layer from sticking. Then I covered the face of the plaster head evenly with the *papier-mâché* mix. It took around 3 to 4 layers to get an even coverage, I waited overnight for the mask to dry and then painted it white and applied paint to look like the heavy make-up of the period.

4   The glasses were a final touch. I am very short-sighted and am always on the look-out for unusual frames. I figure that we wear different clothes most days, so why put the same old boring glasses on day-in and day-out. I particularly like wearing 50s style glasses. On my 50th birthday, a talented designer friend, Susan Holmes, decorated my cake with these cool glasses that she made – a couple of years later they were just perfect for Madame E.

5   Now for a final tip as to how to make the paper ringlets. Just cut recycled paper into approximately ⅓ inch (1 cm) wide strips. Stretch the paper over the sharp blade of a pair of scissors – as if you are working with florist ribbon – and it creates those gorgeous spirals!

Di Jennings

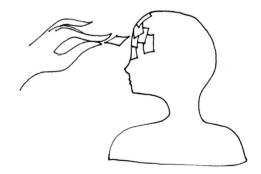

Chapter 6:

Tinsel and Trinkets

‘Surprisingly, it is impossible to feel anything but aloof when wearing this bin bag crown and ring binder bustle ’

Spiralling Elegance

'I SEE YOU GOT YOUR BRAND NEW rubbish bag pill box hat,' quips the bitter bard. Surprisingly, it is impossible to feel anything but slightly aloof when wearing this woven bin bag crown and ring binder bustle. The high class garment made from low class materials lies at the heart of burlesque, summed up succinctly in this get-up for the First Lady from the wrong side of the tracks. In this outfit Di has departed from her usual love of colour-play, indulging instead in a sleek silhouette and suggestive detailing. The ring binders on the hat give height and a line which swoops through the garment, balanced by the binders '*au derriere*'. The confident block shape of the hat is contrasted by the demure netting that shadows the eyes – an accessory which was traditionally favoured by young widows of the elderly elite. Whilst the air of bereavement is carried through with the rigidity of the binders denoting a stiff upper lip, the too-long fish tail flips playfully side to side, a reference to the classic novelty fortune-telling miracle fish, signifying an independent if fickle nature.
Kate MacKay

Design

Back in the 1980s I shared a fashion business with talented New Zealand designer, Kerrie Hughes. We were young and adventurous and delighted in making wacky, over the top creations…and were often surprised when people actually bought them and wore them! Our creations were shown to their best effect in our extravagant and creative fashion shows. One of my favourite memories is a collection of saucy 'Wild West, honky-tonk bar girl'-inspired outfits that were a riot when our models and dancers strutted their stuff on the catwalk. (As I remember an enthusiastic can-can dancer cartwheeled her way right off the catwalk – but it was all part of the fun!) This memory was the initial inspiration for this stylish wee outfit that is made from a charity shop top, black fabric off-cuts and ring binders. That pillbox hat is crocheted from black plastic shopping bags and decorated with a scrap of black net…and more of those gorgeous, spiralling ring binders!
Di Jennings

Materials: pillbox hat

Your recycling

6 glossy black plastic
shopping bags
3 black plastic ring binders
Scrap of netting – fruit and
vegetable bags are good!

Craft supplies

Crochet hook
Needle and thread

Materials: reconstructing

Second-hand stores and hand-me-downs

Assorted garments in
complementary colours and
patterns
Beads, scarfs, trinkets to
accessorise

Craft supplies

Scissors
Needle and thread

TIP:

How to make a pillbox hat from plastic shopping bags

This hat used about six black plastic shopping bags. I used bags that were fairly substantial in terms of their weight and I really like the ones that have a glossy finish. I cut the bags to form a ball of ribbon as explained in 'Summer Collection' (see page 54).

1   The hat is made of two simple shapes – a circle for the top of the hat and a long strip that is joined together to form the brim. I started with the brim by crocheting about ten chain stitches and then worked rows of treble stitches. If you find that your work starts to stick (this is very likely and rather frustrating) try shaking a little talcum powder as you work and it will start to glide through your hands!

2   As you work, check that the band you are working on is the width that you want for the height of your pillbox. If not, adjust the number of stitches accordingly.

3   Continue to work rows of trebles until the strip of crochet is equal to the circumference of your head at the place where you want the hat to sit.

4   Cast off and join the short ends of the strip to form a crown or circle.

5   To make the centre of the hat, make five chain stitches, join them together and work concentric rows of treble stitches into the centre to form a growing circle. You may find that to keep the circle flat you will need to adjust the numbers of trebles in each row. It will be trial and error, but it soon becomes evident just what will work.

6   Cast off when the outer circumference of your circle equals the measurement of the already completed hat brim. Then hand sew the circle to the brim to make the hat.

7   Decorate your hat as you wish. Look around and see what treasures you have in your environment – feathers, beads, scraps of net etc. Or alternatively, leave your creation as a simple pillbox *à la* Jackie Onassis! Although I doubt she ever strutted her stuff in a Wild west bar…

TIP:
Reconstructing charity shop garments

I collect recycled garments when I see them if I love the fabric and the pattern. I am less concerned about the cut/design as I know that I can cut, slash and reconstruct the item to create something entirely new: sleeves can become leggings; a blouse can become a short skirt; long trousers can become pedal pushers…or several simple garments can be reconstructed to create a more complex garment (see the Madame Butterfly project in this chapter for a good example). There are endless possibilities.

1   The secret is to gather garments that complement one another and arrange them intuitively into a new formation. Then cut and slash, pin and stitch.

2   I often attach components together with safety pins and try on the emerging creation before committing to stitching the new look. Safety pins are better than dress-maker's pins for this as they don't stab as you try the garment on!

3   The 'spiralling' dress is a very simple reconstruction. It combines a see-through top from which I removed the sleeves and a sequinned dress that was cut into a mini skirt. Then the two pieces were hand stitched together.

4   To create a slimline effect with the skirt, at the same time as allowing plenty of movement, I have used one of my favourite tricks and inserted a 'godet' at the centre back. This is a half circle of fabric that is sewn into the back seam. The straight edges of the godet are sewn to the straight edges of the back seam (that has been left unstitched from the bottom area to the hemline). The curved edge of the godet becomes the hem and provides plenty of room for a knees up!

Di Jennings

Buckle Pendant

❝ I am interested in transforming
the seemingly-dated object
into something extraordinary,
contemporary and wearable ❞

Buckle Pendant

THE HMONG PEOPLE, from the mountains of southeast Asia, believe that at the very beginnings of the Earth, the land was covered by the sea. Upon this sea sailed a brother and sister, locked inside a yellow, wooden drum – one depiction of the two has them secured by strong bonds.

The Sky People saw that the Earth was in flood, and that the only motion on the water was the yellow drum-ship of the siblings. The King of the Sky ordered holes to be punched into the Earth, so the water would drain, and eventually, the yellow drum struck the ground and shattered their bonds.

The siblings looked about the Earth, dismayed at the barren land, devoid of life. There were no people, only the brother and the sister. The brother scratched his head and had a marvellous idea. He said to his sister:

'All the people are gone. Marry me, we can have children.'

Horrified, the sister replied:

'I can't marry you because we are brother and sister.'

Finally the brother had another wonderful idea. He said, 'Let's carry the grindstones (he had grindstones) up the hill and roll them into the valley. If the stones land on top of each other, then you will be my wife.'

This plan baffled his sister, but intrigued by the sheer insanity of the idea, she agreed. The sister rolled her grindstone and then, with a lurid grin, the brother stepped up and rolled his stone. He then ran down the hill after his stone, he ran as fast as his little legs could carry him, and eventually reached the stones, placing one on top of the other.

The sister wept tears of amazement as she saw the stones atop of each other. She agreed to marry her brother and a year later she gave birth to a baby. However, the baby was not a real baby. It had no arms or legs. It was round. Just like a pumpkin. The brother cut it up and threw the bits all over the place. Wherever they landed, a Clan of Hmong people grew. This was quite splendid. Years later, a Hmong Tribesman discovered an old yellow barrel. It was mottled and riddled with wood-worm. Inside the broken vessel, he found the remains of a leather belt. He took the belt, and fashioned a fine glass buckle that he fixed to it, and he gave it to his sister.

Samuel Odell is an author based in Oxfordshire

Design

Over the years I have amassed a wide collection of vintage beads, buttons and fabrics. I am interested in transforming the seemingly-dated object or fragment into something extraordinary, contemporary and wearable. I think of my work as an alchemic process and take great pleasure in teaching others the techniques and skills to create their own personal and equally extraordinary artwork and to realise their own innate creativity.

My range of jewellery includes pendant and choker necklaces which are made from vintage and contemporary beads and buttons.

I found this lovely buckle in amongst a bag of buttons from a charity shop. I liked the shape and colour and decided to create a very simple but effective pendant necklace to include that anyone can try.

I embellished the buckle by wrapping the surface in silver-plated wire and attached a glass heart bead to the middle. I then simply threaded pink ribbon through the back of the pendant and added smaller matching glass heart beads through the ribbon.

Sarah Galliers

TIP:

How to make a buckle pendant

1   Start by embellishing the buckle itself, wind wire in coils around it, using the wire to thread beads as you go. You can cover the surface in a texture of seed beads or make a feature of an interesting one, as I have done with the lovely heart bead here.

2   Thread the ribbon through the buckle, making a slip-knot for the buckle to hang from the centre. This is the time to check how it hangs and make necessary counterbalancing adjustments. Thread complementary beads along the ribbon, this helps to bring the piece together as a coherent whole.

3   Make a loop from your ribbon at the length you would like your pendant to hang, secure this with a knot to soothe the instant gratification soul or with a little stitching for the eagle-eyed perfectionist. There you go – a simple but effective project. Once you start looking, you realize there are so many different interesting buckle designs and they are great to work with because they already have loops and fixtures to attach things from.

Sarah Galliers

Buckles are great to work with because they already have loops and fixtures to attach things from

Materials

Second-hand stores, jumble sales and hand-me-downs

Belt buckle
Buttons and beads
Ribbon

Craft supplies

Silver plated or copper wire

Pearly Queen

Pearly Queen

IT HAS BEEN SAID, and rightly so, that the true forefather of any Alchemy Artist is none other than the royal highness of lowness himself, Henry Croft, the first ever pearly king. True, indeed, that he knew how to work a bit of cockney alchemy in his day and was well versed in the art of making his own luck and fortune from bits and pieces that others passed by. So one day, down by the Thames looking for some luck or a laugh, Henry Croft finds something better than both. There on the riverbank, brighter than silver, more beautiful than gold; a gleaming shoal of pearly buttons, set adrift off a boat from Japan.

Henry filled his pockets, he filled his hat and began to sew, stitch and thread while the lamps were lit and became again dark and the sun sank and rose. Birds and flowers, and stars and spirals of pearly-white glistened on his old black whistle and flute (suit) so he looked like a one-man travelling fair. Decked out so from his hat to his toes, Henry Croft walked proudly down The Strand to where the costermongers sold their wares. So heavy was the weight of a thousand pearly buttons and so weary did they make him that he took off his hat and set it on the ground. With a great cheer, the market crowd poured forth to fill his hat with pennies and shillings until it overflowed with good fortune. So the line of pearly royalty began; the kings and queens sewing pearl-covered whistle and flutes for their pearly princes and princesses and handing down their own suits as treasured heirlooms. To this day, every London borough has its very own pearly king and queen who lift local spirits and raise money for charities.

One such man is George Major, the pearly king of Peckham, who first told me the story of Henry Croft and the pearly ancestry. Abandoned by his mother, George was seven years old when he found out he was in fact a pearly prince. Perhaps it was the buttons in his blood that led young George to set about transforming harsh reality into gold. With quick wits and sheer determination, he survived an abusive father and a terrifying aunt. George would sell his neighbours' fences as firewood to buy food for himself and his sisters; with white-washed cauliflowers and jars full of 'Genuine London Smog' he plied his trade, never letting the odd court hearing deter him.

It was his neighbour Iris who made George his first pearly suit. Despite arthritis she stitched through the nights, determined that George should claim his pearly inheritance. In that suit he would visit his sister Violet, collecting money in his tin for the hospital where she stayed, and so he began his life and work re-stitching realities to become a true button king, bettering his own life by bettering others. But we all know that the life of a royal is thwarted with controversy and the pearly regency is no exception. Torn between family feuds and questionable kinships, banished from the Lord Mayor's parade, his beloved Cockney Museum now closed, George advises thus: if you see a man or a woman adorned in buttons, and want to know if they are a true pearly, think of Henry Croft walking to market, setting down his hat to crowds of applause. Then look at the man or woman before you and you'll see for yourself.

Kate MacKay

www.pearlykingofpeckham.com

Design

Oh, swoon… I have been dreaming of the button-embellished… I have buttons! A whole jar of them! Then I remember an old Ann Taylor Loft denim skirt somewhere in my closet that I haven't worn in years (I don't know why – it is pretty cute without embellishment). I have decided to put my own stamp on it, reinvent it and wear it again. I have gathered my notions and inspiration: my denim skirt, the sea of buttons, beautiful pictures from magazines and art books. I have positioned myself with all these lovely things around me and stare and stare until I have figured out my plan of action.

It's very simple – and SUCH an easy project! Really, no real sewing skills are required here. You are just putting on buttons. A whole lot of them! Even with strategic button planning and placement, there were gaps. I had a remedy for this. I filled in the spaces with French knots – fear not the French knot! Then I added a running stitch from the button-clusters to the hem…

Carrie Sommers

Materials

Second-hand stores, jumble sales and hand-me-downs

Plain skirt in dark fabric
Pearl buttons

Craft supplies

Embroidery thread
Scissors and needle

TIP:

How to embroider a French knot

OK. Onto the French knot or, as some of you have started referring to them, the dreaded French knot. Really, they aren't *that* bad.

1   To start, bring your thread to the front. Hold the thread firmly between your left index finger and thumb and away from the fabric.

2   With the needle pointed away from the fabric, wrap the thread over and around the needle with your left hand. Wrapping twice will give you a smaller knot; three times will give you a larger one.

3   Holding the thread taut with your left hand, turn the needle downward and start to take it to the back a few threads away. (If you try to use the same hole, the knot is very likely to pull back through and disappear.) With the tip of the needle inside the hole, slide the knot down the needle onto the fabric pulling the thread taut with your left hand at the same time. This is where the tension comes in. If you pull the knot too tightly, the eye of the needle won't fit through the knot as the thread goes to the back. If it's too loose you'll get a sloppy knot that won't lay flat.

4   Slowly push the needle to the back of the fabric while holding the knot in place under your thumb. I usually hold the *thread* down with my thumb because it helps to see the knot. Begin to pull the thread through. Continue to pull until the thread disappears under your thumb and is completely pulled through.

Janet McCaffery

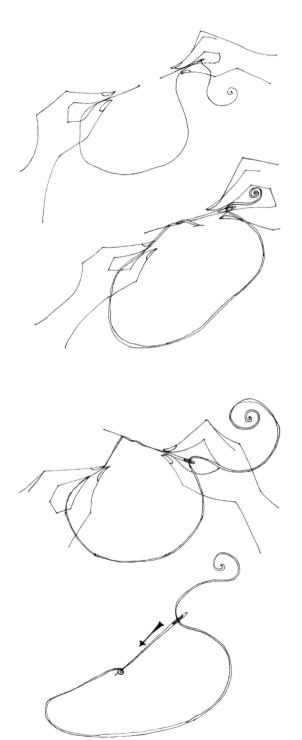

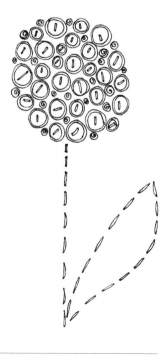

Fill gaps between buttons with French knots, then add a running stitch from the buttons to the hem

Phoenix Charms

Phoenix Charms

THE ISLAND OF ST KILDA is shaped like a giant stone apple core. Cliffs arch more than a thousand metres on each side, reaching up out of the cold and cruel North Sea. When the first settlers reached St Kilda it was a mountain, with beaches that sloped gently up to the summit. But, over time, the punishing sea scratched and scraped, hacked and chiselled, swallowing its beaches, until only the centre was left. If you took a boat to St Kilda today, you would see a kilometre-high tower of rock with a grassy table top; shaped just like I said, a huge stone apple core.

Now, when people lived on St Kilda, they would rarely make it down to the sea, as the overhanging cliffs were so dangerous to climb. As a result they could never fish in the sea, and as they had no livestock they relied on crops and the eggs of the swallows that cluttered the nooks and crannies of the cliff faces. The swallows gathered here in their multitude, chirping busily as they darted and danced upon the ocean's thermals. For years the islanders lived in harmony with the swallows, their relationship balanced perfectly like a ballet dancer on her toes. For every egg the swallows would lay to hatch a chick, another would be laid to be given to the islanders, so that they could feed their children. In exchange for eggs, the islanders would grow the finest of crops, and give half to the swallows, so that they could feed their chicks and make nests from the straw.

For many generations the islanders adhered to this ancient pact, but as with so many things, greed got the better of them. Soon the relationship lost its balance, stumbled and collapsed onto the ground never to pirouette again. It occurred to one of the islanders that he could suspend himself off the cliff face with rope, allowing him to steal extra eggs straight from the nests of the small birds. Soon all the islanders were abseiling down the cliffs, and egg after egg after egg was being stolen. The ancient pact of trust had been broken. As soon as a swallow laid an egg, it was taken; a swallow chick destined to be born, would be turned into an islander's dinner. For a year and a day, not a single swallow chick was born. Still the islanders stole more and more eggs, while their children grew fat and sleepy. The swallows were owed children by the islanders, soon the day came when this debt would have to be settled: an eye for an eye, a tooth for a tooth. The swallows flew far out to sea; taking huge breaths as they dived deep into the ocean where rubies lined the beds. Clutching the jewels tightly in their beaks, each swallow carried a single ruby to the surface. In silent formation, under the guard of nightfall, the flock returned for one last time to their island.

While the greedy, full-bellied islanders slept, swallow-after-swallow flew into bedroom-after-bedroom. In every throat of every child a single ruby was placed. These rubies were no ordinary rubies though, they had the extraordinary ability to rewrite wrongs and readjust balances. The following morning the islanders were woken by the screams of every mother and father; for lying in each child's bed was no longer a child, but instead a chirping, fluttering swallow, with a red glowing throat. The swallows left the island that day taking the swallow children with them. The debt had been repaid, much to the dismay of the islanders.

To this day you can always tell which swallows are actually human children, by the red mark on their throat from the ruby that they carry.

Will Brownlie

Design

Initially inspired by the changeability of nature I was attracted to gems which reflect and change with the light such as moonstones which resemble the sky, with luminous blues, opaque clouds and sudden flashes of rainbows. Labradorite or black moonstone resembles the deep green sea or a dark forest. I often base the decision of what I wear on what I see that morning; if I see sparkling rain on leaves my jewellery must be silver and green, a bright blue grey sea calls for an opal, amber comes out on golden autumn days.

Since starting to recreate items of jewellery from remnants, gifts and some purchases from craft suppliers, I have mostly made items for myself which are often very personal. For this project I decided to complete something I had been intending to do for some time: combine healing and jewellery making, my two base skills, to create a gift for someone else. The magnetic bracelet evolved from the challenge to find something nice but age-appropriate for a ninety-year-old lady. I had noticed, at work, many older people looking for long necklaces they could easily slip over their heads or bangles with no awkward clasps for arthritic hands. This bracelet is made from magnetic hematite beads, which are said to have pain relieving properties, plus assorted beads and trinkets from broken and discarded jewellery. It is designed to be easily put on, difficult to loosen but then also easy to take off. I took into account the recipient's personal likes and dislikes, which accounts for the green stones from Iona.

Crystals and gemstones are becoming widely used for their healing properties by trained therapists as well as sold in shops for specific ailments and conditions. Many people may wish to create a personalised bracelet or necklace, for a specific healing purpose, as a gift or for their own use, but the large amount of complicated and often conflicting information on the subject can make this seem a daunting task. Isn't tiger's eye too energizing for this ailment? Or malachite too calming? Should I also consult the zodiac? Garnet and jade are both recommended but they clash! My advice, when preparing a healing gift, is to trust in your intuition and whichever jewels you are drawn to will most likely be right. Your intention is the most important thing so examine it carefully. To devote time and thought into making something you know your friend will like will also make them feel good, as long as you check for sharp edges or loose wire which can undo all of your good work.

Annie MacKay

TIP:
How to source your healing charms

The beads used to create this bracelet all came from old and discarded jewellery. The magnetic Hematite beads came from a necklace bought in a charity shop, as did the hand made green beads and the gold coloured beads. The smaller green beads are Tourmaline from another necklace and the dragonfly and leaf trinkets are from old earrings. Charity shops are treasure troves for old beads, the jewellery often being old, out of fashion but not yet antique so quite cheap. You can also be lucky and find gold and silver chains for new pendants. I have occasionally bought a cheap chain and bead necklace, removed the plain beads with pliers and replaced them with rose quartz or moonstones. Over time I have outgrown certain jewellery or it has gone out of style so it is ideal for recycling. I had a coral and river pearl necklace and bracelet set, strung with small gold beads, which had been left unworn for years until inspiration came along. I restrung it, replaced the gold beads with silver ones, made it shorter, added a silver dragonfly pendant, from an old earring and then had a special gift for one of my daughters.

Once people know that you make jewellery you will find that they will give you their unused or broken jewellery to recycle. My daughters often buy me interesting pieces from charity shops as gifts to fuel the jewellery factory. On rare occasions I have received things given to a friend by an 'ex', really nice pieces which for obvious reasons the person did not wish to keep. On receiving this type of item remember the three golden rules:

1   Never ask questions!

2   Wait until you are sure they won't get back together before using the piece.

3   Wait until you are sure that the 'ex' won't be elevated to the status of fondly-regarded 'old flame'. There is no time limit on that one!

My tip is to keep it safe and be ready to discreetly return it as you got it.

Once people know that you make jewellery they will give you unused or broken items to recycle

Materials

Second-hand stores, jumble sales and hand-me-downs

Assorted jewellery, interesting beads, lone earrings, charms and trinkets
2 ¾ yards (2.5 m) of 24 gauge (½ mm) silver wire, strong nylon or plastic thread
A closed jump ring and an open jump ring

Craft supplies

Scissors
Wire cutters
Flat-nosed pliers – for dismantling old jewellery
Round-nosed pliers
Ruler or tape measure
Optional – a magnifying light can be very helpful for those of us with weakening eyesight or poor lighting in the work area

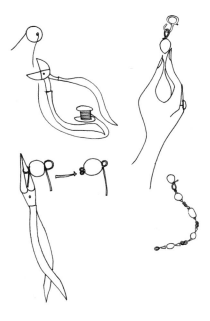

TIP:

How to make a new necklace rise from the ashes of the old

1 Lay the beads out against a ruler to ensure you have the right quantity for the desired length. Whilst you are doing this you will inevitably find you change the design around a few times but make sure you leave a ³⁄₁₆ inch or 4mm gap between the beads. You can you use a specialist necklace mould but I find a ruler does fine.

2 Thread the first bead of the necklace on to the wire so that you have approximately ½ inch or 1½ cm out of one end. Bend the wire to one side at a right angle to the bead. Then repeat on the other side leaving ½ inch or 1½ cm in wire, then snip with the wire cutters at those lengths.

3 Using the round-nosed pliers wrap the wire into a loop by the bead leaving the remaining wire pointing outwards. Repeat to the other side of the bead.

4 Still using the round-nosed pliers hold the looped wire firmly on one side with one hand and using the snipe/chain-nosed pliers with the other hand wrap the wire around the base of the loop.

5 Tuck the remaining wire into a tidy, spring-like shape.

6 Repeat these stages, 1 to 5, on one side of each bead except the last one.

7 Hook the beads together by linking the finished end of one bead to the unfinished end of the next.

8 If you are satisfied with the style and length (I never am), complete wrapping the wire of the unfinished side of each bead into a loop as in Step 4.

9 Use the jump ring and bolt ring to make a clasp. Hook the jump ring onto the unfinished end of the necklace and wrap the wire around the loop as in Step 4.

10 Find the small cut in the open bolt ring and twist it to make a gap, then hook it onto the other end of the necklace. Using pliers close the gap in the bolt ring.

11 Check for stray pieces of wire sticking out of the necklace and tidy them away. Final adjustments can be made to the necklace by unpicking it with pliers to shorten by removing a segment or lengthen it by inserting extra sections. Do not forget to check again for sharp wire sticking out.

12 Wear and enjoy.

Annie MacKay

Charity shops are treasure troves for jewellery which is out of fashion but not yet antique, so quite cheap

Frida Headdress

❛An icon of Mexican art and
a woman of strange beauty,
Frida Kahlo is a great
inspiration❜

Frida Headdress

AS AN ICON OF MEXICAN ART and a woman of strange beauty, Frida Kahlo is a great inspiration to many of our designers. She is in her work as she was in life, constantly struggling between harsh realities and dreamlike escapism.

A macabre fiesta that is frightening and alluring; Frida Kahlo knew the power of adornment, in fact it could be said that she adorned herself in power. Crowned in flowers, twisted spirals of black hair scraped up and woven with blood red ribbons, she was ornamented with defiance. Dripping with talismans of life and swathed in the colours of celebration she armoured herself against pain. Her body became an extension of her canvas – and then the canvas itself on which to paint the layers of her world, imagined, hoped for and feared. She paraded through life like a carnival procession, a statue robed with such intent that she would be able always to express her history and innermost secrets in a single gesture. She made herself a walking icon of Mexican identity, standing with the stature of one who wears the weight of the collective memory on their back.

Her body – unravelling at the seams – and her tortured heart were soothed and contained beneath attire that was almost ceremonial. Like the smooth steady pace of her brush strokes that so opposed the tormented content of her work, her adornment was unwavering, too perfect even and unsettlingly still. She painted herself into becoming all that she wanted to be; steadily, methodically on canvas and in life. In her self-portraits the scrutiny of detail is such that it moves towards the surreal. Her eyebrows are swallows, her necklace is thorns and the decorative foliage is at once distant and integral to the braids of her hair. It is as if everything she experiences – actions, thoughts and dreams – are spun into the garments that she wears. Ordinary moments are twisted with history, embroidered with memories, embellished with hopes and loves then stitched into an ornamental rag doll wearing a floral crown, a colourful scarf and a trailing pleated skirt.
Kate MacKay

Design

It's important to play. It came so easily when we were children…we didn't have to 'work up to it' or feel that we 'deserved it'. We just played. So that's what I did one morning. One of my favorite books in terms of gaining-inspiration is *Self Portrait in a Velvet Dress: The Fashion of Frida Kahlo* (2008). It includes colour photos of Frida Kahlo's personal wardrobe and accessories. So today I pretended that my vintage dress was for Frida and dressed her in some of my favorite things.

I started of course with a heavily embroidered Mexican *huipil* blouse that I had purchased on my trip to Oaxaca and a Guatemalan skirt from a yard sale. This I embellished with an embroidered cotton apron from the Alameda flea market and a ruffled underskirt from a thrift store. These beautiful embodiments of feminine Mexico were the iconic dress with which Frida masked the casts and disfigurements of her injured body. To adorn her further, I added a pendant designed by an artist in San Miguel de Allende hung from a heavy silver necklace that I've had forever. For the finishing Frida-esque touch, I added a flamboyant headpiece which I designed to go with a wedding dress I made last fall.

Did you know that Diego Rivera stipulated a period of fifty years from the moment of Frida Kahlo's death until her bathroom/dressing room in Casa Azul could be opened? In April 2004, the director of the Frida Kahlo museum opened Frida's locked door and began the painstaking job of restoring her wardrobe and personal effects. (The project was documented in the aforementioned book.)
Lori Marsha

TIP:

How to transform a headband into a headdress

The structure of a headdress can be challenging to make. If I am making an outfit for the stage I sometimes want to create a large scale headpiece for theatrical effect. It is a challenge to find materials that are light enough to be worn on the head without giving the poor model or actress a headache. I find that a large, finely woven bag can be an excellent starting point. It is light and flexible and can be moulded into different shapes.

1　A good starting point for adventures in hair adornment is to embellish an existing hairband. Find one that is quite sturdy and not likely to snap, remember those horrific padded ones from the 80s? Time to look them out, don't worry about the pattern – it will all get covered up!

2　Use thin wire to secure your decorative elements, a good source for this is florist suppliers. Wind on your fake flowers, Christmas decorations, feathers, onion netting – I have a fondness for a single pendant hung on the forehead, a potential new lease of life for a favourite earring that has lost its mate.

3　Wind scarves and strips of fabric or lace around to cover the unsightly original hair band and also to protect the head from jaggy bits of wire and bumpy bits and bobs.

4　Finish with a string of beads or some dangling ribbons.

Di Jennings

Materials

Second-hand stores, jumble sales and hand-me-downs

Sturdy plastic headband
Fabric scarves
Ribbons, feathers and trimming
Trinkets and beads

Craft supplies

Thin wire, such as florist wire
Needle and thread

Madame
Butterfly

❝ In the spirit of the armchair
traveller, our oriental phoenix
rises from the ashes of a
Scottish scrap store ❞

Madame Butterfly

AS RUDYARD KIPLING, who visited Japan in 1899, wrote: 'Verily, Japan is a great people, her masons play with stone, her carpenters with wood, her smiths with iron and her artists with life. Mercifully, she has been denied the last touch of firmness in her character that would enable her to play with the whole round world. We possess that. We, the nation of the glass flower shade, the pink worsted mat and the red-green china puppy doll and the poisonous Brussels carpet. It is our compensation.'

When Britain finally got its hands on the markets of East Asia, it was received with the good grace and respect which only an imperialist nation is capable. When romantic fantasies of the 'exotic East' collided with new realities, myths bred with stereotypes and a mutant art movement was born. No-one could deny that the typical rose-flocked, gold-trimmed, varnished and *decoupaged chaise-longue*-come-gentleman's-desk suddenly seemed somewhat heavy-handed beside the delicate craftsmanship of Japanese carving or subtle glaze of Chinese ceramics. However, with the optimism of the arrogant, Britain began to get stuck in to making its own 'Oriental art'.

Willow pattern production began in the factories of Shropshire, spawning a frillier offspring of its Chinese uncle. The new minimalist aesthetic was lapped up by the Victorian gentry. In fact, the insatiable thirst for Zen paraphernalia was such that once every soup tureen, pickle castor, cake stand and knife rest had been embellished with crinoline-enhanced Orientals, the globally-aware gent began on the wallpaper. Now, the markets of East Asia did not provide wallpaper per se, but undeterred British traders realised that just a little opium could get you quite a lot of Chinese prints if you bought them in bulk. These could be varnished straight to the wall, in a veritable cacophony of calligraphy. The policy 'less is more' did not concern the fashionable Victorian. How better to fully appreciate the fine lines and muted wash of a Chinese print than to fully saturate yourself in the medium from the comfort of your knick-knacked drawing room? It is in the spirit of the armchair traveller that our Oriental phoenix rises from the ashes of a Scottish scrap store. Kimono sleeves from paisley patterned ties, embroidered sash from sofa cushions, topped off with a bin bag and beanie hat headdress.
Kate MacKay

Design

This outfit was such fun to make…and to photograph. I just love the make-up! I started by trawling through my collections to create a 'sea of stuff' with an Oriental feel. Deep red was the predominant colour, with intricate patterns that worked together in interesting ways.

The under garment is made of three tops that have been re-fashioned and joined together to form a long dress. The cumber band is made from placemats and is overlaid with a separate belt made of woven ties. The kimono is made from many elements including an old silk petticoat, scarves, ties, fans and a hat. The headpiece is fashioned from plastic bags and discarded jewellery/ bits 'n' bobs.

The tie was just asking to be woven to form a belt. At first I wasn't sure how to make the headdress, but woke up one morning and started playing with black plastic bags and it became obvious how to progress. I love both the shape and the decoration. I collect jewellery from jumble sales and markets and seem to have a never-ending supply of broken bits. I have stopped cursing when I lose an earring because I know that the remaining one will find a home in one of my creations when the time is right!

Di Jennings

Second-hand stores, jumble sales and hand-me-downs

6 ties

Craft supplies

Hooks and eyes
Needle and thread

Play with colour and pattern as you weave and pin the ties into place

TIP:

How to make the belt from woven ties

1   I chose 6 ties with small geometric patterns in maroons, reds and blues. I used three ties for the warp (long pieces) and another 3 for the weft (short pieces that are woven through).

2   I cut the ties at the point where the narrow part starts to widen out. You will not use the wide part of the ties – but how about saving them as the inspiration for another creation? Then I cut the remaining ties into short lengths, ensuring that I added sufficient allowances to weave through the warps and attach to back of the belt.

3   First I laid out the long ties parallel to one another. Then I started weaving through with the shorter lengths. I suggest that you start about 2 inches (5 cm) from the V-shaped end of the ties as this will create an attractive overlap for fastening the belt when you have finished weaving. Enjoy playing with colour and pattern as you weave and pin the ties into place. I found that I altered the positioning of the different wefts a few times before the colours and patterns were positioned just how I wanted them.

4   To ensure that the belt was stable I turned it over onto the back and hand stitched the wefts to the warps at random intervals. Don't stitch it in too many places – the weaving is best left as flexible as possible. Then I turned the belt over to the back and hand stitched the raw ends at the end of the belt. You could create a lining to cover the back of the belt. But I left mine as it is – after all, we are recycling here and this work does not have to be about a perfect finish. No need to be a neatness freak! Finish your beautiful belt by attaching large hooks and eyes to fasten it – this can be worn at back, front or the side. Play and have fun!

Since making this belt I have thought of many more applications for woven ties – they would make a fabulous front panel for a jacket, a cushion cover or even a beautiful wall hanging.

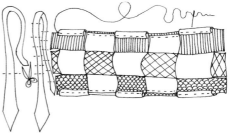

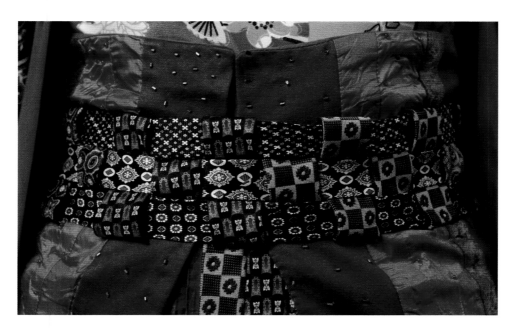

Materials

Second-hand stores, jumble sales and hand-me-downs

1 stretch woollen hat/beanie
6 black plastic ring binders
Discarded jewellery bits 'n' bobs for decoration

Your recycling

2 large black plastic bags
15 lightweight plastic bags for stuffing (any colour)

Craft supplies

Scissors
Needle and thread

TIP:
How to make the geisha-look headdress

My philosophy is to use what is cast off in my immediate environment, rather than going out hunting for materials. This way the design is informed by the materials available rather than the other way around. Granted I am something of a magpie and collect bits and pieces at charity shops and jumble sales that catch my eye – and I am fortunate in having access to the Alchemy Arts scrap store that is an Aladdin's Cave of discarded fabric. But sometimes the materials I want just come my way before I even know I am going to need them – sheer serendipity!

I had picked up a beanie hat in a cable car while I was on a holiday and was unable to find the owner so I brought it home, and washed it thinking my son may want it. He did not – he is pretty choosy about his hats – but I laid my hands on it as I was thinking through how to make this headdress and found that the beanie made the perfect base to build it on.

1   I made a rough drawing of the hat and the shapes that I would need to create it. I then cut 2 circles from the black plastic bags. The circumference of the bigger circle is about twice the measurement of the beanie at the brim when it is stretched on the head. I hand gathered the perimeter of the circle of plastic and then hand sewed it to the brim of the beanie, leaving a gap of about 2⅓ inch (6 cm) unstitched. Then I stuffed the hat with plastic bags until I got the desired shape and hand sewed the 'gap' in place.

2   For the top part of the hat, I cut a smaller circle from a black plastic bag and hand gathered the perimeter as above. It seemed to me that the hat would need reinforcing before I attached the second tier, as plastic can rip readily. So before attaching the 'bun' to the top of the hat, I found a stronger piece of black plastic and cut a circle about 4¾ inches (12 cm) in diameter that I then glued to the centre of the hat to reinforce it. Then I attached the smaller circle of plastic to this reinforced area and went through the same process as above – stuffing with plastic bags and hand sewing the 'gap' into place.

3 This work is pretty experimental and I found that the hat was sitting too high at the nape of the neck. So I cut black ring binders to look like ringlets and attached them to the back of the hat to sit at the nape of the neck. Apparent mistakes can frequently lead to creative solutions!

4 Now for the fun bit – I am always oh-so-happy when the main construction is complete and I can fiddle about with decoration. I gathered some broken bits of jewellery and pinned them to the hat in various combinations until I was happy with the overall look – and then hand sewed them to the hat. I also used a crocheted plastic flower that was left over from the 'Hula' outfit.

Pin broken bits of jewellery to the hat to complete the look

Sheriff Badges

‘ I liked the absurdity of Wild
West badges made out of soft,
bendy foil – the very opposite
of dangerous! ’

Sheriff Badges

QUESTION! WHAT HAPPENED TO BIG NOSE GEORGE PARROT?!! Answer! Well, he ended up as a pair of boots and a bag and a doorstop. Crikey to Betsy! That sure is a peculiar answer, partner. With an all-American, apple pie slice of the gruesome and a star-spangled banner of the grizzly, the story of Big Nose George puts the 'golly' in 'gosh' and the 'cor' in 'blimey'! Pour me another red eye, slide it down the bar, tell Sam to play another tune on the *pee-anna* and I will begin the ghastly tale… Let me tell you something this ain't mere *taradiddles* (Western slang for a traveller's yarn), this tale is the truth, with less lies in it than you would find on a priest's poker face…

In the 1800s in Carbon County, there was no greater band of outlaws than the cattle rustling, train robbing, sheriff murdering 'James Gang'. Like a pack of wild coyotes these brothers rode across the prairies leaving a trail of bastards and widows. Now, George Manuse (or Big Nose George Parrot as he was called on account of his large nose) somehow got mixed-up with these renegade land pirates. It was a failed attempt to rob a train that ended George's career. Although the James Boys escaped, George was captured. He was sentenced to be hung. In prison in Rawlins, Wyoming, George beat the guard within an inch of his life and attempted to escape – '*He sure was one bad owl hoot…*' When news of George's violence reached the local community a lynch mob stormed the prison and strung him up from a pole outside the Fred Wolfe Saloon.

Death is where most people's story ends, but in the case of Big Nose George, this is where his macabre saga begins. A local doctor, Dr Osborne, was given possession of his body. First he sawed open George's head to see if his brain was any different to law abidin' folk. Alas, he found no signs of the devil. He kindly gave the top of his skull to Dr Lillian Nelson, Wyoming's first female doctor. One can only imagine her excitement at receiving such a generous present. As we all know, girls like nothing more than the top of an outlaw's skull. Apparently she used it as a bespoke door stop.

Next, Dr Osborne instructed George's body to be skinned. He sent the hide to a tanner in Denver with the instructions that he wanted George's chest to be made into a pair of boots, requesting that the nipples were kept as a prominent design feature. Even then, Dr Osborne understood the importance of accessorizing correctly, and as such he also requested that George's back be turned into a medical bag. He obviously knew that matching an accessory with one's shoes can really lift an outfit, and that there is no stronger matching combo than shoes and a bag. (In this instance, topping it off with a hat would perhaps be too much.)

The story of Big Nose George Parrot has taught me that I want to lead a law-abiding lifestyle. I am now making a consistent effort to stop robbing trains and stealing cows; I implore to you to do the same before you turn into a pair of nipple boots. I now wear a sheriff badge so everyone knows which side of the tracks I stand.

Will Brownlie

Design

I like to promote my work directly to the public through craft fairs and events and specialist parties in Scotland as I enjoy discussing it with random folk as well as other makers in the same field. I am happy to disclose the processes involved in creating each piece of work as this promotes a general dialogue about recycling. This can bring about an exchange of ideas and sometimes reawaken memories of skills I'd thought forgotten.

The sheriff badges came about as a result of being invited to an acoustic evening with an American Western theme. I wanted to provide something that would help me to fit in, using recycled materials. I have two hungry cats at home and they eat their way through several foil cat food trays per week. Some of the trays are gold or silver in colour. These seemed the perfect material to make some sheriff and revolver badges.

Sarah Galliers

240

TIP:
How to make a sheriff badge

I used a cat food tray but of course any foil packaging will do, just make sure it's empty and clean.

1 Draw a Sheriff Badge shape and design on one side of the soft foil using a ball point pen. (Use the pen nib firmly over the surface.) Have fun embellishing this with swirls and designs, write quotes or personalise with the name of a person or the event. You can do other shapes too, for this Wild West event I made mini pistol badges too, I liked the absurdity of a gun made out of soft bendy foil and fabric – the very opposite of dangerous!

2 Turn the foil over to the right side to reveal an effective embossed surface. (Remember to write any words in reverse.) Carefully cut the badge shape out (edges are sharp).

3 Using your cut-out as a guide, make a slightly larger sheriff badge shape on two scrap bits of fabric. Machine stitch around these with a zig-zag stitch leaving a ⅓ inch (1cm) gap at the end. Stuff this to make a little cushion pad with a bit of scrap wadding and sew the remaining gap up.

4 Machine stitch the embossed silver star badge onto the surface of the cushion with a zig-zag stitch, allow the stitching to be part of the design by selecting the colour accordingly.

5 Finally, complete by sewing a metal brooch back onto the reverse side.

Sarah Galliers

Materials

Your recycling

Cat food trays or other foil packaging in silver or gold

Second-hand stores, jumble sales and hand-me-downs

Scraps of fabric
Buttons and beads
Brooch pin

Craft supplies

Ball point pen
Scissors
Needle and colourful threads
Domestic sewing machine

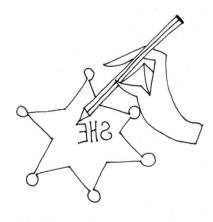

Christmas Fairy

A truly fun and festive
costume for Christmas parties,
street parades and festivals!

Christmas Fairy

TWELFTH NIGHT IS THE TRADITIONAL DATE for the 'Wassailing procession' in southern England. Villagers would process from home-to-home bearing tidings of good health and bowls of potently alcoholic Wassail. The procession would be lead by the Pine Lady, a kind of hybrid Burry man (pagan plant spirit/May queen type). The Pine Lady's attire would have been handed to her from a long line of Pine Lady ancestry. The whole outfit from the hat to the shoes was made of prickly pines, incredibly painful to wear and not at all attractive. Each household would hang a coin or silver trinket on her branches and share a dram with the Pine Lady as a gesture of wealth and health for the coming year. Of course as the night went on the Pine Lady would become progressively inebriated and her garbs increasingly heavy, having to be held up and led by a group of patient attendees. A martyr to her cause, her life-expectancy was short and her dignity non-existent. Women's lib, plastic pines and raised hemlines have made life a whole lot simpler for the modern Pine Lady. Dubbed the 'Pine Ladette' in recent years by some disapproving traditionalists, to be a Pine Lady is now the most coveted of roles in the British country calendar.

The pine element of the dress is now relatively minor, pictured here in a provocative and flirtatious mini skirt of plastic fir. The heavy coins have been replaced by light baubles and tinsel in racy red and gold. The increased wearability of attire, together with the Pine Lady's inherited ability to handle a drink means that it can now take up to five consecutive days of Wassailing before a typical English village will get any sleep.

Kate MacKay

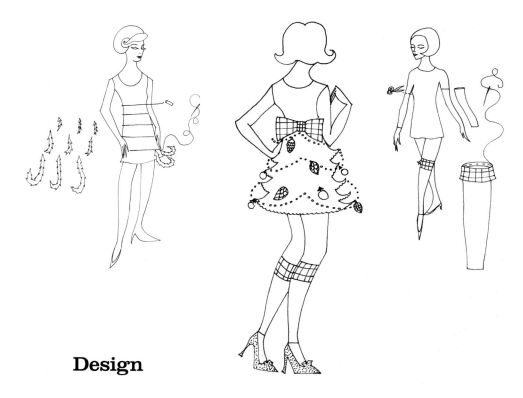

Design

Christmas is such a beautiful time. I love all the twinkling lights, the colourful decorations and the air of festivity. When December comes around I can't wait to get the Christmas tree up and start decorating the house. But after Christmas is over, there is so much waste. So it felt great to recycle some of that Christmas excess. As I was moving countries (yet again!) and did not plan to take our Christmas tree with me, I decided to transform it into a fun costume. Our Christmas fairy is made from this discarded artificial Christmas tree, various decorations and tartan fabric scraps from Alchemy Arts' scrap store. The headpiece was inspired by my door wreath. Scottish folk do such wonderful Christmas decorations – that added touch of tartan is just perfect!

I used an old long-sleeved jersey tunic as the base for this creation. I cut the branches from the tree, divided them into lengths and hand sewed them to the tunic in rows, with the shorter branches at the top graduating to the longer branches at the bottom.

I particularly like the leggings that were made from the tunic sleeves – they are more wearable than the festive dress that is great fun but does require great care when you are sitting down to avoid crushing the ornaments!

Di Jennings

Materials: leggings

Second-hand stores, jumble sales and hand-me-downs

Cut off sleeves (stretchy fabric)
Tartan fabric scrap

Craft supplies

1 metre of ⅓ inch (1cm) wide elastic
Scissors, needle and thread

Materials: frock

Second-hand stores, jumble sales and hand-me-downs

Discarded fake Christmas tree
Tunic made from stretchy fabric
Tartan fabric scraps
Christmas rosettes and baubles

Craft supplies

Wire cutters
Needle and thread

TIP:

How to make a pair of leggings from sleeves

1 Choose a top that is made from a stretchy knit fabric.

2 Cut the sleeves off at the underarm in a straight line. Try them on your legs. Mine came to just above the knee and fitted perfectly.

3 If the fit is not quite right, turn the 'leggings' inside out and pin, then stitch and slash seam allowances as required – the beauty of knits is that they do not readily unravel. To finish the top of the leggings I added a band of tartan. I used just one layer so as not to create bulk and used the natural selvedge to form the lower edge of the band.

4 If the leggings tend to fall down, use a circle of elastic, about ⅓ inch (1cm) wide, to hold them up. Make the elastic into a circle using the same method as the tartan band described above and stitch in place between the tartan band and the top of the legging. Attach by hand sewing in 3 or 4 places only to maintain the stretch. I finished the leggings with a Christmas bow at the sides. Use your imagination – look in your trinket box for broken earrings, old ribbons…whatever rocks your socks! And then dance those legs out to some Christmas parties!

TIP:

How to make a frock from a Christmas tree

1   I started on this project by cutting all the branches from the central pole of the tree with wire cutters.

2   Then I divided the branches into 3 groups: short, medium and long. I used a stretchy tunic top that had seen better days and marked a horizontal line in dressmaker's chalk just below the bust.

3   Then I marked positions on the line about 1¼ inches (3cm) apart to show where I wanted to attach the branches.

4   At this stage I decided that it would be simplest to start attaching the branches at the bottom of the tunic first to avoid them getting tangled up as I worked. I marked more rows on the tunic and made dot marks to show where to attach all the branches.

5   Once the tunic was all marked up, the thinking part was mainly over. It was then just a matter of hand-stitching the branches to the tunic. I started at the bottom of the tunic and hand-sewed the top of each branch individually as marked. I used the longest branches at the bottom, the medium branches in the middle area and

the shortest ones at the top – this created an attractive tree-shaped silhouette.

6   I find that when I am designing, I usually think through the silhouette that I want to create first. The detail in terms of pattern, texture and decoration usually comes later. In this case, I played with Christmas rosettes and placed them in a pleasing pattern to create an interesting bust line, pinning and then hand sewing them into place.

7   I added a tartan sash with a wee bow at the back, and draped some long ropes of Christmas bead like decorations under the bust to create a bordello kind of look.

8   The final touch was to attach the decorations to the branches. This is a truly fun and festive costume for Christmas parties, street parades and festivals!

Di Jennings

Look in your trinket box for broken earrings, old ribbons...whatever rocks your socks!

Alchemy Artists' Profiles

Kay Farnie

I live and create my work in Edinburgh's seaside town of Portobello. The local charity shops and jumble sales are a rich source of the bold and quirky retro items which I love to design with. I am a collector of vintage garments that catch my eye for their unusual style, bold patterning and contrasting colours. Eventually my hoard spills over into local art markets where I sell them together with items I have reworked, refashioned and created from bits and pieces that intrigue and inspire.

Elaine M Huang

I'm a computer scientist living in Aachen, Germany. Originally from New York, I did my undergrad just outside of Philadelphia and my PhD in Atlanta and have also lived in Chicago and the Bay Area. My hobbies are dance, sewing, crochet, knitting, playing piano, learning languages, snuggling my cats and baking. I love 1950s evening gowns and collect lots of them and patterns too. I enjoy thinking about design and colour and texture and how to alter patterns to realise an idea that I have in my head.
www.burdastyle.com/member/elainemay

Kerrie Hughes

My career as a fashion designer started in Wellington, New Zealand. This is where I met fellow designer and long time friend, Di Jennings. We shared a love of edgy and unusual design and liked to entertain others with our creative and fun designs.

In London, together with designer Penny Meachin, we created our label Idol. I currently live in New Zealand where I work as an independent artist and designer. I have always been interested in clothing as a means of self-expression and concentrate on hand crafted techniques, creating garments that cannot be mass-produced.

Di Jennings

My diverse career has involved working in fashion design, wearable art, the film industry, community development and community arts. Personal, planetary and creative transformation all hold a fascination for me. The latter has developed into a love of a creative process in which I gather diverse materials and elements from my environment and transform them into something that is much more than the sum of the individual parts. For me, this process is even more valuable when carried out by a group and when each member brings their own talents and perspective to a collaborative creative process.

Sarah Kay-Wren Galliers

I have made crafts and textiles since my youth and delight in using the materials I have to hand. I originally trained as a knitwear designer in the 1980s. I diversified into interior design promoting both printed and knitted textiles throughout the UK through craft and trade fairs and specialist shops. I became involved in community art projects in 2001 from a desire to work with others creatively. With a growing interest and concern for environmental issues, I have developed a range of art work and textiles to a high standard with a minimum impact on the environment and with a low cost of production.
www.kaywren.co.uk

Knitty Kitty

Knitty Kitty is Edinburgh-based, Dublin-born Catherine Walsh
I remix wool and plastic like a recycling DJ: blending my mother's crafty and father's resourceful genes.

I have been referred to as 'The Queen of the Thrift Shop': thriving on the thrill of textile finds, tools and trimmings in car boot and jumble sale hunts, raids on bargain bins and friends' cast-offs piles. From these I reincarnate clothing and accessories. I'm an eternal child and collector with a particular penchant for nostalgia and fun.
www.knittykitty.org.uk

Cynthia Korzekwa

It was a desire for change that convinced me to leave Texas and move to Italy in search of *La Dolce Vita*. That's how I became a permanent foreigner. Luckily, I've had my art because making art is like having a portable home – when you create, you create not only objects but a personal universe as well. A place where you belong.

At present, I'm working on a book, *Muy Marottage*, that focuses on recycled clothing, because we always need clothes.
www.housewife.splinder.com / www.cynthiakorzekwa.org

Annie MacKay

I am an ex-nurse with creative flair who is currently working in a village shop which sells Fair Trade foodstuffs, jewellery, crafts and alternative books. My creativity used to be channelled into the home, decorating hanging pictures and constantly moving furniture around, but to my husband's relief I discovered jewellery.

Throughout history, it seems that people from all over the world have adorned themselves with jewellery to denote something about their lives. This inspired me to explore beliefs and symbols of ancient civilisations and cultures, also the magical and spiritual significance of certain ornaments.

Fi MacKay

I had been working within the independent boutiques of Edinburgh for a number of years and, wanting to explore a hobby that pushed my understanding of fashion, enrolled in a dress making evening class. Here I discovered a love of crafting and constructing clothes which led me to pursue a full-time Costume Design course.

I adore fashion, photography and design and am influenced by the abundance of independent designers and boutique owners within Scotland's capital city. I love seeing how my grandmother's style evolved throughout the 1950s and 60s in period photographs and recognising the influence these garments have on fashion today.
www.kiss-on-the-lips.blogspot.com

Kate MacKay

I grew up in South London, part of an incredibly fun and creative family. As far back as I can remember I was developing a love of stories, illustrations, making things, dressing up, imagining and adventuring. Having London's wealth of second-hand bookshops and markets on my doorstep, as well as buskers, parades and free parties, instilled in me a sense of creative abundance; there were always things happening to excite and inspire.

It must have been my attraction towards the artists, storytellers, materials and places on the fringes of society that led me to develop the Alchemy Arts scrap store and art studio in Edinburgh's seaside town Portobello.
www.spanglefish.com/katemackayfineart

Janet McCaffrey

I began by creating pillows from my extensive collection of vintage haberdashery. It was a great stress-reliever from a high-pressure job. After realizing that this was way more fun than my full-time job, I decided to follow my heart and devote more time to this new venture.

My pillows have been described as fabric collages, with layer-upon-layer of materials. I generally work with bright colours in unusual combinations and love to mix patterns – plaids with polka dots, stripes with graphic florals. Mostly I love carrying on the tradition of fine needlework in a way that combines the best of old and new.

www.primrosedesign.com

Jo McCall

I am a recent graduate of Textile Design from Heriot Watt Universities School of Textiles and Design. I have had a life-long love of collecting tat of all kinds and hoard all manner of fabrics and materials for crafting purposes.

My collections have always been focused on eco-friendly production and combining my own knitting with recycled products. I have become involved with freelance community art and design projects in Edinburgh that encourage people to recycle and consider the environment, as well as being involved in youth work and volunteer Art Therapy.

Lori Marsha

Some find their fashion aesthetic in the malls of America, others in flea markets or obscure on-line shopping categories. My reworked designs are another alternative. I sell my work in a variety of venues from a funky shop on Olvera Street in LA to The Smithsonian's Renwick Gallery in Washington DC. I'm proud of those accomplishments but my true joy comes in making an individual person happy to have stumbled across my work.

www.lorimarsha.com

Carrie Sommers

I am the owner of Sommer Designs LLC – I design and create a line of hand crafted women's accessories in my home studio in Southern California. I enjoy sewing and knitting, creating beautiful things to wear and adorn my home. My love of thrifting and antiquing sees me collecting unusual materials to use in my work. Bargain designer, antique buttons and scraps of lace are all collected until inspiration strikes.

My creations are available on my website, at select boutiques in the US and at local craft events in the Southern California area.

www.sommerdesigns.com

Index

Conversion Tables

LENGTH

1 inch = 2.54 centimetres = 25.4 millimetres

KNITTING NEEDLES SIZE GUIDE

Metric (mm)	3	4	5	6	7	8	9	10	12
UK	11	8	6	4	2	0	00	000	—
US	—	6	8	10	—	11	13	15	17

CROCHET HOOKS SIZE GUIDE

Metric (mm)	2	2.25	2.5	2.75	3	3.75	4	4.5	5	5.5
UK	14	13	12	—	11	—	8	7	6	5
US	—	B/1	—	C/2	—	F/5	G/6	7	H/8	I/9

Acknowledgments

Thank you so much to all the artists across the globe who have so willingly and enthusiastically shared their knowledge, ideas and inspiration. It is this generosity and abundance of art that allows creativity to thrive for generations.

Thanks to those who bravely modelled for us in the cold winter studio; all independent and creative women: Bex Robinson, Cecilia Stamp, Fi MacKay, Cara Hind, Rosie Lewis, Knitty Kitty, Sophie Buckingham and especially Edda Kjarval whose geisha make-up took the longest!

Thank you to Out of the Blue Arts Trust and Go Reborn Collective for allowing us to take photographs in their beautiful gallery spaces. Thank you to Bits and Bobs scrap store and Carnival Chaos Productions who I'm sure recognise many of the materials they have donated to us over the years. Finally, thanks to Waste Aware Edinburgh for their continued support of Alchemy Arts projects and endeavours.